THE ULTIMATE GEN

Z

A-Z DICTIONARY

How To Communicate And Master The Slangs Of The Youngest And Most Influential Generation

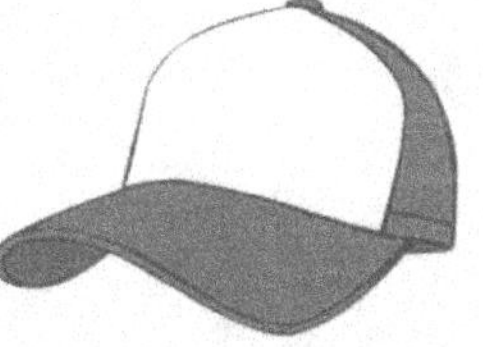

JASON KING

Contents

INTRODUCTION

Hey there! Ever wondered what makes the younger generation tick? Well, it's time to dive into the fascinating world of Gen Z slangs and unlock a whole new level of connection and understanding!

In a world where communication is always changing, and each new generation has its own unique way of speaking, currently, it's Generation Z that is taking the lead.

Here's a scenario that shows how the Gen Z (a.k.a Zoomers) slangs reigns supreme at an alarming rate in this ever-evolving world and why it's important to be conversant with this lingo.

In a bustling tech store,a young gamer storms in, frustration etched across his face as he recounts his disastrous gaming experience from the night before,due to his slow gaming pc . With unwavering determination, he approaches the sales clerks, yearning for an upgrade to his precious PC.

But here's where things gets interesting. This young, tech-savvy lad,being the hip Gen Z soul that he is,unleashes a fury of Gen Z slangs in his plea for an upgrade.

Gamer: *"Yo, I need a major upgrade, pronto! My rig's been hella laggy, and it totally wrecked my Call of Duty sesh last night. I need some fire!"*

But oh! Woe is him as the two clueless sales clerks,lost in a sea of confusion,are utterly incapable of comprehending the linguistic maze this lad was spewing.Instead they recommended all the wrong items oblivious to the gamer's needs.

Of course,the poor gamer was furious! He expected understanding,dammit!His eyes was glowing as he glared at the two clerks in front of him, clenching his fist fiercely.

Gamer: *"Nah, that ain't it! I need something that's absolutely chill, like iconic drip. My graphics card needs to slap! I need something that won't leave me shaking as I wanna be a whole ass snack when I'm in the zone"*

He slapped his palm on the wall with a force that startled the clerks

They both scrunch their faces, utterly taken aback and pausing in their tracks just to think for a moment. With errs,they still recommended totally different items.

"Err…do you need a snack?" it was the lady clerk that asked " *or um maybe a juice or a loaf of bread, I think these will make you chill while in the zone"* the guy clerk gestured.

Guy Clerk:"You seem lost, maybe I should recommend you a grocery store just two blocks away, as we don't sell these here".

The young gamer, now utterly confused and starting to get more furious, gestures emphatically to express his discontent. His face completely fell , no mask of coping left. His eyes keep wandering, feet moving faster until he ran out of breath

Gamer:"*what the actual eff,you muffins? This ain't what I'm looking for! Seriously, y'all not getting it, y'all ain't getting it, y'all making me go cray cray*"

He smoldered with rage flowing through him like hot lava

The clerks became more confused and started stunting profusely as they'd tried calming down this strange guy.

luckily for them, Just when all hope seem lost, a savior emerges from the shadows -another employee, **Adam**, who possess the rare skill of the Gen Z slang comprehension catches wind of the conversation, he grin slyly as he step forward to assist, smirking.

Adam:(nodding confidently to the young gamer)*"Yo, got you covered, my man! Check out this absolute zdaddy of rigs! It's the one that'll give your setup the iconic drip you're after. And the graphics card on this beast? It'll slap so hard, you won't even remember the word 'lag'!"*

Gamer:(excited and relieved)*"Finally! That's exactly what I need!"*

With a proud smirk, Adam glances back at the other bewildered clerks, showcasing his understanding of Gen Z slang.

Adam: *"You know, guys, understanding Gen Z slang has its perks. It helps me connect with customers on a whole new level. That's why I've got the edge and an extra paycheck to my name."*

And thus, dear reader, the scene transitions seamlessly into the grand introduction of ***"The Ultimate Gen Z A-Z Dictionary."***

This comprehensive guide ensures you evade the plight of the uninformed clerks. In a world dominated by Gen Z slang, this book empowers you with the linguistic tools required to engage with today's influential youth.

In a world where communication transcends traditional boundaries, mastering Gen Z slang has become paramount to understanding the pulse of today's youth. The scenario witnessed in the tech store reflects the ever-growing language barrier between generations.

The two sales clerks unable to comprehend the Gamer's Gen Z lingo, exemplify the gap in communication that many individuals face today. As the world evolves, so does its language, and failing to keep up can lead to misunderstandings and missed opportunities for connection.

"The Ultimate Gen Z A-Z Dictionary" serves as a beacon for those seeking to bridge this linguistic divide. It's not just a dictionary; it's a roadmap to understanding and engaging with the youngest and most influential generation. Within these pages lie the keys to unlocking a vibrant, ever-evolving lexicon that defines the Gen Z culture.

This book isn't merely a compilation of words; it's a journey into a world where "yeet," "sus," and "iconic drip" are more than phrases; they're symbols of identity and expression. By grasping these linguistic nuances, readers will equip themselves to communicate effortlessly, relate authentically, and connect meaningfully with the youth of today.

In a landscape where language shapes perception, this book becomes an essential tool for those seeking not just communication but genuine understanding in an evolving world dominated by Gen Z slang.

Let's Speak Gen Z

A

AF - Pronounced as "A-F"

> *Meaning:* Abbreviation for "as f**k," used to emphasize something strongly.
>
> *Usage:* "This party is boring AF."

A1 - Pronounced as "A-one"

> *Meaning:* Top quality or excellent.
>
> *Usage:* "That restaurant serves A1 food."

Adorbs - Pronounced as "uh-dorbs"

> *Meaning:* Adorable or cute.
>
> *Usage:* "Your puppy is absolutely adorbs."

Adulting - Pronounced as "uh-dult-ing"

> *Meaning:* Acting like an adult or handling responsibilities.
>
> *Usage:* "I spent the weekend adulting, doing laundry and paying bills."

Ain't nobody got time for that - Pronounced as "Aint nobah-dee got tym fuh that"

> ***Meaning:*** Expression indicating a lack of interest or time for something.

> ***Usage:*** "Sorry, ain't nobody got time for drama."

All good - Pronounced as "awl good"

> ***Meaning:*** Everything is okay or fine.

> ***Usage:*** "No worries, it's all good."

Amazeballs - Pronounced as "uh-maze-balls"

> ***Meaning:*** Amazing or awesome.

> ***Usage:*** "The concert last night was totally amazeballs."

And I oop - Pronounced as "and eye oop"

> ***Meaning:*** Reaction to a surprising or awkward situation (originated from a viral video).

> ***Usage:*** "And I oop, I didn't mean to do that!"

Antisocial social club - Pronounced as "an-tee-soh-shuhl soh-shuhl kluhb"

Meaning: Someone who prefers solitude but may also enjoy socializing in small doses.

Usage: "He's part of the antisocial social club, preferring Netflix over parties."

ATM - Pronounced as "ay-tee-em"

Meaning: At the moment.

Usage: "Can't talk, busy ATM."

Awks - Pronounced as "awks"

Meaning: Abbreviation for "awkward," used to describe uncomfortable or embarrassing situations.

Usage: "That was so awks."

AYFKM - Pronounced as "A-Y-F-K-M"

Meaning: Abbreviation for "Are you f***ing kidding me?"

Usage: "AYFKM? That's unbelievable!"

AYFR - Pronounced as "A-Y-F-R"

Meaning: Abbreviation for "Are you for real?" or "Absolutely, for sure."

Usage: "AYFR, that's insane!"

AYOO - Pronounced as "A-Y-OO"

Meaning: Abbreviation for "Are you okay?"

Usage: "You fell, AYOO?"

AYYY - Pronounced as "A-Y-Y-Y"

Meaning: Expression of excitement or agreement.

Usage: "AYYY, that's awesome!"

As if! - Pronounced as "Az if"

Meaning: Expression of disbelief or disagreement.

Usage: "You think I'd do that? As if!"

All the feels - Pronounced as "awl thuh feels"

Meaning: Experience intense emotions or sentimental feelings.

Usage: "That movie gave me all the feels."

And chill - Pronounced as "and chil"

> *Meaning:* Suggesting to relax or calm down.

> *Usage:* "Take a breath and chill."

Alt - Pronounced as "awlt"

> *Meaning:* Short for "alternative," often used in online communities to refer to different or non-mainstream ideas.

> *Usage:* "That's a more alt perspective."

Aight - Pronounced as "eye-t"

> *Meaning:* Slang for "alright."

> *Usage:* "I'll see you later, aight?"

AFAIC - Pronounced as "A-F-A-I-C"

> *Meaning:* Abbreviation for "As far as I'm concerned."

> *Usage:* "AFAIC, that's the best place to eat."

AFAIR - Pronounced as "A-F-A-I-R"

> *Meaning:* Abbreviation for "As far as I remember" or "As far as I recall."

> *Usage:* "AFAIR, that's what happened."

Ah-mazing - Pronounced as "Ah-may-zing"

> *Meaning:* Variation of "amazing," used to describe something fantastic.

> *Usage:* "That dessert was ah-mazing."

Ahoy - Pronounced as "ah-hoi"

> *Meaning:* A greeting or an attention-getting word (originating from nautical terms).

> *Usage:* "Ahoy! How's it going?"

Airhead - Pronounced as "air-hed"

> *Meaning:* A person perceived to be unintelligent or lacking common sense.

> *Usage:* "He's such an airhead sometimes."

Ate - Pronounced as "eyt"

> *Meaning:* Used to describe someone who is fashionable or stylish.

> *Usage:* "She's always so ate."

Awoo - Pronounced as "uh-woo"

> *Meaning:* A howling sound expressing excitement or happiness.

> *Usage:* "We heard a loud awoo from the crowd."

Aww - Pronounced as "aw"

> ***Meaning:*** Expression of sympathy or endearment.

> ***Usage:*** "Aww, that's sweet of you."

AYT - Pronounced as "A-Y-T"

> ***Meaning:*** Abbreviation for "Are you there?"

> ***Usage:*** "I'm waiting for your response, AYT?"

LAP - Pronounced as "A-L-A-P"

> ***Meaning:*** Abbreviation for "As late as possible."

> ***Usage:*** "Submit the report ALAP."

All-nighter - Pronounced as "awl-nai-ter"

> ***Meaning:*** Staying awake or working through the entire night.

> ***Usage:*** "I had to pull an all-nighter to finish the project."

Aces - Pronounced as "ey-siz"

> ***Meaning:*** Excellent or top-notch.

Usage: "You did an aces job on that project."

Ahellnah - Pronounced as "uh-hel-nah"

Meaning: Expression of strong disagreement or refusal.

Usage: "Ahellnah, I'm not doing that."

Airdrop - Pronounced as "air-drop"

Meaning: Sharing files or photos wirelessly between devices.

Usage: "I'll airdrop you the pictures."

AFAIU - Pronounced as "A-F-A-I-U"

Meaning: Abbreviation for "As far as I understand."

Usage: "AFAIU, we're meeting at 3."

AOK - Pronounced as "A-O-K"

Meaning: Abbreviation for "All okay" or "All good."

Usage: "Everything's AOK."

AYCE - Pronounced as "A-Y-C-E"

Meaning: Abbreviation for "All you can eat."

Usage: "The buffet is AYCE."

ATW - Pronounced as "A-T-W"

Meaning: Abbreviation for "All the way."

Usage: "I support you ATW."

AO - Pronounced as "A-O"

Meaning: Annoying orange, used to refer to someone or something annoying.

Usage: "Stop being such an AO."

Ah - Pronounced as "ah"

Meaning: Expression of realization or understanding.

Usage: "Ah, now I get it."

Asfs - Pronounced as "Az f***ing soon"

Meaning: Abbreviation for "As f***ing soon."

Usage: "I need it done asfs."

Awesome sauce - Pronounced as "awe-suhm saws"

Meaning: Extremely awesome or excellent.

Usage: "That's awesome sauce!"

Auditioning - Pronounced as "aw-di-shuh-ning"

Meaning: Trying to impress or gain someone's attention.

Usage: "Stop auditioning for him."

Asshole tax - Pronounced as "ass-hohl taks"

Meaning: Paying extra for being unpleasant or rude (informal).

Usage: "He charged him the asshole tax for being rude."

A1 since Day 1 - Pronounced as "A-one since Day one"

Meaning: To be the same or unchanged since the beginning.

Usage: "She's been A1 since Day 1."

AWOL - Pronounced as "ay-wohl"

Meaning: Absent without leave; missing or gone.

Usage: "He went AWOL after the argument."

Amenities - Pronounced as "uh-men-uh-tees"

Meaning: Referring to attractive physical features of someone.

Usage: "He's got some serious amenities."

A-game - Pronounced as "A-game"

> *Meaning:* Giving the best effort or performance.

> *Usage:* "Bring your A-game to the presentation."

A-OK - Pronounced as "A-O-Kay"

> *Meaning:* Everything is fine or okay.

> *Usage:* "The situation is A-OK."

Anchor baby - Pronounced as "ang-ker bey-bee"

> *Meaning:* A child born in a country to non-citizen parents.

> *Usage:* "She's considered an anchor baby."

Ain't - Pronounced as "Aint"

> *Meaning:* Contraction for "am not," "is not," or "are not."

> *Usage:* "I ain't gonna do that."

Aunt Flo - Pronounced as "awnt floh"

> *Meaning:* Euphemism for menstruation or one's period.

> *Usage:* "She's dealing with Aunt Flo."

A-list - Pronounced as "A-list"

Meaning: Referring to individuals who are at the top of their field or highly regarded in society.

Usage: "He's part of the A-list crowd."

Auto - Pronounced as "aw-toh"

Meaning: Automatically or self-regulated.

Usage: "The system works on auto."

A-ight - Pronounced as "A-yt"

Meaning: Alright or okay.

Usage: "He said everything's A-ight."

All the way live - Pronounced as "awl thuh way lahyv"

Meaning: Something is exciting, happening, or at its best.

Usage: "The concert was all the way live!"

All dat - Pronounced as "awl dat"

Meaning: Describes something as excellent or impressive.

Usage: "She's got it all dat!"

B

Bae - Pronounced as "bay"

• Meaning: Term of endearment for someone special, short for "before anyone else."

• Usage: "She's my bae."

Basic - Pronounced as "bay-sik"

• Meaning: Conforming to trends or stereotypes, lacking originality or individuality.

• Usage: "She's so basic with her fashion choices."

Bless up - Pronounced as "bless uhp"

• Meaning: A positive affirmation, wishing someone well or acknowledging success.

• Usage: "Bless up for acing the exam!"

Bounce - Pronounced as "bouns"

• Meaning: To leave or depart from a place quickly.

• Usage: "Let's bounce from this party."

Bruh - Pronounced as "bruh"

• Meaning: Term used between friends, equivalent to "bro" or "dude."

• Usage: "Bruh, did you see that?"

Bye Felicia - Pronounced as "bahy fuh-lee-shuh"

• Meaning: Dismissive farewell to someone unimportant or irrelevant.

• Usage: "She kept talking, so I said 'bye Felicia'."

Ballin' - Pronounced as "bawl-in"

• Meaning: Having a lavish or luxurious lifestyle, often associated with wealth or success.

• Usage: "He's been ballin' since his promotion."

Beat - Pronounced as "beet"

• Meaning: Tired or exhausted.

• Usage: "I'm so beat after that workout."

Bet - Pronounced as "bet"

• Meaning: Agreement or confirmation.

• Usage: "Let's meet at 6?" "Bet."

Blessed - Pronounced as "blehsd"

• Meaning: Feeling fortunate or grateful for something.

• Usage: "I'm blessed to have such good friends."

Booked - Pronounced as "bookt"

• Meaning: Having plans or being busy.

• Usage: "Sorry, I'm booked all day."

Boomer - Pronounced as "boo-mer"

• Meaning: Refers to someone from an older generation, often used derogatorily.

• Usage: "My boss is such a boomer, he doesn't understand technology."

Bop - Pronounced as "bawp"

• Meaning: A catchy or enjoyable song.

• Usage: "This song is a bop, I can't stop listening to it."

Boujee - Pronounced as "boo-zhee"

• Meaning: Luxurious or high-class, often used to describe someone or something as extravagant.

• Usage: "She's so boujee with her taste in fashion."

Brew - Pronounced as "broo"

• Meaning: Coffee or tea.

• Usage: "I need a hot brew to wake up."

Bro - Pronounced as "broh"

• Meaning: Informal term for a male friend or companion.

• Usage: "What's up, bro?"

Brr - Pronounced as "bur"

• Meaning: Expression of being cold or chilly.

• Usage: "It's so cold, brr!"

Buffering - Pronounced as "buff-er-ing"

• Meaning: Taking time or delayed, often in internet-related contexts.

• Usage: "My video is buffering, it's so slow."

Burn - Pronounced as "burn"

• Meaning: Insult or comeback directed at someone.

• Usage: "That was a sick burn!"

Buzzkill - Pronounced as "buhz-kill"

• Meaning: Something or someone that ruins a fun or exciting moment.

• Usage: "Don't be a buzzkill, let's enjoy the party."

BYOB - Pronounced as "bee-why-oh-bee"

• Meaning: Abbreviation for "Bring Your Own Booze" or "Bring Your Own Bottle."

• Usage: "The party's BYOB, remember to bring your own drinks."

Baddie - Pronounced as "bad-ee"

• Meaning: A confident and attractive person.

• Usage: "She's a total baddie in that outfit."

Banger - Pronounced as "bang-er"

• Meaning: A great or exciting event, song, or experience.

• Usage: "Last night's party was a banger."

Betrayed - Pronounced as "buh-treyd"

• Meaning: Feeling deceived or let down by someone.

• Usage: "I felt so betrayed when he lied to me."

Big mood - Pronounced as "big mood"

• Meaning: Expression used to agree or emphasize with someone's feelings or sentiments.

• Usage: "Your frustration with that is a big mood."

Big facts - Pronounced as "big fakts"

• Meaning: Acknowledging something as true or agreeing strongly.

• Usage: "What you said is big facts."

Blackout - Pronounced as "blak-out"

• Meaning: Loss of memory due to excessive alcohol consumption.

• Usage: "I had a blackout after those shots."

Blow up - Pronounced as "bloh up"

• Meaning: To become very popular or gain attention suddenly.

• Usage: "Her TikTok video blew up overnight."

Bounce back - Pronounced as "bouns bak"

• Meaning: To recover or return to a good condition after a setback or difficulty.

• Usage: "I know you'll bounce back from this."

Brain fart - Pronounced as "breyn fart"

• Meaning: Temporary mental lapse or forgetfulness.

• Usage: "Sorry, I just had a brain fart."

Break the internet - Pronounced as "breyk thuh in-ter-net"

• Meaning: Something so viral or popular that it overwhelms internet traffic.

• Usage: "Her post might break the internet."

Brick - Pronounced as "brik"

• Meaning: Extremely cold weather.

• Usage: "It's brick outside."

Bread - Pronounced as "bred"

• Meaning: Money or cash.

• Usage: "I'm making bread at my new job."

Bump - Pronounced as "buhmp"

- Meaning: To play loud music or a song.

- Usage: "Let's bump some tunes."

Bruh moment - Pronounced as "bruh moh-muhnt"

- Meaning: An embarrassing or awkward situation.

- Usage: "That was a major bruh moment."

Bubble guts - Pronounced as "buhb-uhl guhts"

- Meaning: Feeling of intestinal discomfort or stomachache.

- Usage: "I ate too much, now I have bubble guts."

Buff - Pronounced as "buhf"

- Meaning: Physically fit or muscular.

- Usage: "He's been working out, looking buff."

Bug - Pronounced as "buhg"

- Meaning: To annoy or irritate someone.

- Usage: "Stop bugging me."

Built different - Pronounced as "bilt dif-ernt"

• Meaning: Being unique or having a different perspective.

• Usage: "She's built different from the others."

Bullet - Pronounced as "buh-let"

• Meaning: A speed or performance measurement.

• Usage: "The car has a top bullet."

Bummed - Pronounced as "buhmd"

• Meaning: Feeling disappointed or unhappy.

• Usage: "I'm bummed I couldn't make it."

Bust down - Pronounced as "buhst doun"

• Meaning: Someone who is promiscuous or flamboyant.

• Usage: "She's a bust down."

Butthurt - Pronounced as "buht-hurt"

• Meaning: Feeling overly offended or upset over something trivial.

• Usage: "He's so butthurt about losing the game."

BYE - Pronounced as "bahy"

• Meaning: An exclamation used to dismiss someone or something.

• Usage: "BYE, I'm done with this conversation."

Bathroom break - Pronounced as "bath-room breyk"

• Meaning: A pause or break, often used humorously in social situations.

• Usage: "I need a bathroom break from this meeting."

Buzzy - Pronounced as "buhz-ee"

• Meaning: Feeling excited or stimulated.

• Usage: "The atmosphere was buzzy at the concert."

Backseat gaming - Pronounced as "bak-seet gay-ming"

• Meaning: Giving unwanted advice or instructions while someone else plays a video game.

• Usage: "Stop backseat gaming, let me play."

Bail - Pronounced as "beyl"

• Meaning: To cancel plans or not show up.

• Usage: "I had to bail on the party."

Bandwidth - Pronounced as "band-width"

• Meaning: Emotional or mental capacity to deal with something.

• Usage: "I don't have the bandwidth for this right now."

Bang for the buck - Pronounced as "bang fawr thuh buhk"

• Meaning: Getting the best value for money spent.

• Usage: "That product has great bang for the buck."

Bangin' - Pronounced as "bang-in"

• Meaning: Excellent or impressive.

• Usage: "The food at that restaurant is bangin'."

Bank - Pronounced as "bank"

• Meaning: To have a lot of something.

• Usage: "He's got bank in his account."

Bask in - Pronounced as "bask in"

• Meaning: To revel or enjoy something fully.

• Usage: "Let's bask in the moment."

Bay - Pronounced as "bay"

• Meaning: A term of endearment for someone special, short for "babe."

• Usage: "Hey bay, how are you doing?"

C

Cap - Pronounced as "kap"

Meaning: To lie or exaggerate.

Usage: "He's capping about his achievements."

Chill - Pronounced as "chil"

Meaning: To relax or calm down.

Usage: "Just chill, everything will be okay."

Clout - Pronounced as "klout"

Meaning: Influence or power, especially on social media.

Usage: "She has a lot of clout online."

Cringe - Pronounced as "krinj"

Meaning: Feeling uncomfortable or embarrassed by something.

Usage: "That video was so cringe."

Cray cray - Pronounced as "kray kray"

Meaning: Extremely crazy or insane.

Usage: "Last night's party was cray cray."

Cya - Pronounced as "see-ya"

Meaning: Abbreviation for "See you."

Usage: "Cya later!"

Curate - Pronounced as "kyoo-reyt"

Meaning: To select, organize, and present content or information.

Usage: "I'm curating my Instagram feed."

Curve - Pronounced as "kerv"

Meaning: To reject or ignore someone romantically.

Usage: "She curved his advances."

Cheugy - Pronounced as "choo-gee"

Meaning: Outdated, unfashionable, or trying too hard.

Usage: "Wearing mom jeans is so cheugy."

Clap back - Pronounced as "klap bak"

Meaning: Responding to criticism or insults in a sharp and confident manner.

Usage: "She had the best clap back to his comments."

Capisce - Pronounced as "ka-pee-sh"

Meaning: Italian term meaning "understand" or "got it."

Usage: "We're meeting at 6, capisce?"

Crypto - Pronounced as "krip-toh"

Meaning: Cryptocurrency or digital currency.

Usage: "He invested in crypto."

Cuck - Pronounced as "kuhk"

Meaning: A derogatory term for someone considered weak or submissive.

Usage: (Note: This term is offensive and derogatory.)

Cake - Pronounced as "keyk"

Meaning: Money.

Usage: "I'm making cake at my new job."

Chonky - Pronounced as "chon-kee"

Meaning: Fat or overweight, usually used humorously.

Usage: "Look at that chonky cat!"

Cuffed - Pronounced as "kuhft"

Meaning: Being in a committed relationship.

Usage: "They're cuffed since last summer."

Catfish - Pronounced as "kat-fish"

Meaning: To deceive someone by pretending to be someone else online.

Usage: "I think she's getting catfished."

Caked up - Pronounced as "keykt uhp"

Meaning: Having a lot of money or being wealthy.

Usage: "He's caked up after his successful business."

Canceled - Pronounced as "kan-suhld"

Meaning: To reject or discontinue support for someone or something due to their actions or behavior.

Usage: "He got canceled for his controversial remarks."

Check yourself - Pronounced as "chek yer-self"

Meaning: Reflect on your behavior or attitude.

Usage: "You need to check yourself before talking to others."

Chillax - Pronounced as "chil-laks"

Meaning: Combining "chill" and "relax," meaning to calm down or take it easy.

Usage: "Chillax, it's not a big deal."

Clutch - Pronounced as "kluch"

Meaning: To be extremely useful or helpful in a critical situation.

Usage: "Your advice was clutch."

Caking - Pronounced as "key-king"

Meaning: Spending a lot of time with a romantic partner.

Usage: "They've been caking all weekend."

Cha-ching - Pronounced as "chuh-ching"

Meaning: The sound of a cash register, often used to express making money or success.

Usage: "She just got a promotion, cha-ching!"

Chill pill - Pronounced as "chil pil"

Meaning: Calm down or relax.

Usage: "Take a chill pill, it's not that serious."

Crumbs - Pronounced as "krumz"

Meaning: A small amount of money.

Usage: "I've only got crumbs left until payday."

Chirp - Pronounced as "churp"

Meaning: To insult or mock someone.

Usage: "Stop chirping at him."

Cut it - Pronounced as "kut it"

Meaning: Stop doing something or cease an action.

Usage: "Just cut it, I've had enough."

Crash - Pronounced as "krash"

Meaning: To unexpectedly fall asleep.

Usage: "I crashed after the long day at work."

Chillin' like a villain - Pronounced as "chil-in lahyk uh vil-in"

Meaning: Relaxing or being at ease, often used humorously.

Usage: "I'm just chillin' like a villain."

Cool beans - Pronounced as "kul beenz"

Meaning: An expression of approval or agreement.

Usage: "Cool beans, I'm glad you liked it."

Chirpse - Pronounced as "churps"

Meaning: Flirting or engaging romantically with someone.

Usage: "He's chirpsing that girl at the party."

Cheesin' - Pronounced as "chee-zin"

Meaning: Smiling broadly or happily.

Usage: "She's cheesin' in every picture."

Craic - Pronounced as "krak"

Meaning: Fun or enjoyable times, often used in Ireland.

Usage: "We had great craic at the party."

Chip on the shoulder - Pronounced as "chip on thuh shoh-ler"

Meaning: Holding a grudge or carrying resentment.

Usage: "He's got a chip on his shoulder about the argument."

Cray-cray - Pronounced as "kray-kray"

Meaning: Extremely crazy or insane.

Usage: "Last night's party was cray-cray."

Compliment bomb - Pronounced as "kom-pluh-muhnt bom"

Meaning: Giving multiple compliments to someone at once.

Usage: "She dropped a compliment bomb on her friend."

Chopped - Pronounced as "chawpt"

Meaning: Drunk or intoxicated.

Usage: "He was completely chopped after the party."

Cloud - Pronounced as "kloud"

Meaning: Reputation or fame, especially online.

Usage: "He gained a lot of cloud after the viral video."

Cupcaking - Pronounced as "kuhp-key-king"

Meaning: Excessively displaying affection in public, especially between couples.

Cop - Pronounced as "kop"

Meaning: To obtain or acquire something, often used in reference to buying or getting something.

Usage: "I'm gonna cop those sneakers."

Cuffing season - Pronounced as "kuhf-ing see-zuhn"

Meaning: The time during the colder months when people seek a romantic partner to spend time with.

Usage: "It's cuffing season, time to find someone to cuddle."

Cheddar - Pronounced as "cheh-duhr"

Meaning: Money or cash.

Usage: "He's making cheddar at his new job."

Chump - Pronounced as "chuhmp"

Meaning: A foolish or gullible person.

Usage: "Don't be a chump, think before you act."

Capped - Pronounced as "kapt"

Meaning: To be surpassed or beaten.

Usage: "We capped our sales target for the month."

Crusty - Pronounced as "kruhs-tee"

Meaning: Unkempt, dirty, or unpleasant.

Usage: "That old jacket looks crusty."

Cringe-worthy - Pronounced as "krinj-wur-thee"

Meaning: Describing something so embarrassing or uncomfortable that it makes you cringe.

Usage: "The speech was cringe-worthy."

Cuz - Pronounced as "kuhz"

Meaning: Shortened form of "because," often used informally.

Usage: "I couldn't make it cuz I had other plans."

D

Dope - Pronounced as "dohp"

Meaning: Cool or excellent.

Usage: "That new song is dope!"

Dead - Pronounced as "ded"

Meaning: Something boring or without life.

Usage: "The party was dead."

Dank - Pronounced as "dank"

Meaning: High-quality or excellent.

Usage: "These memes are so dank."

Drip - Pronounced as "drip"

Meaning: Fashionable or stylish clothing or accessories.

Usage: "He's got so much drip with those shoes."

Dub - Pronounced as "duhb"

Meaning: A loss or failure.

Usage: "Taking that exam was a dub."

Deadass - Pronounced as "ded-ass"

Meaning: To be serious or truthful.

Usage: "I'm deadass about this."

DYEL - Pronounced as "dye-el"

Meaning: Abbreviation for "Do you even lift?"

Usage: "DYEL? Your muscles look big!"

Darty - Pronounced as "dahr-tee"

Meaning: A daytime party.

Usage: "Let's hit that darty this weekend."

Dank - Pronounced as "dank"

Meaning: High-quality or excellent.

Usage: "These memes are so dank."

Dope - Pronounced as "dohp"

Meaning: Cool or excellent.

Usage: "That new song is dope!"

Deets - Pronounced as "deets"

Meaning: Details.

Usage: "Give me the deets on the event."

DRM - Pronounced as "dee-ahr-em"

Meaning: Abbreviation for "Doesn't Really Matter."

Usage: "DRM, I'll go anyway."

Dubs - Pronounced as "duhbz"

Meaning: Wheels or rims on a car.

Usage: "He's got dubs on his ride."

Darty - Pronounced as "dahr-tee"

Meaning: A daytime party.

Usage: "Let's hit that darty this weekend."

Dip - Pronounced as "dip"

Meaning: To leave or depart from a place.

Usage: "I'm gonna dip, see you later."

Dime - Pronounced as "dahym"

Meaning: A perfect ten or an attractive person.

Usage: "She's a dime."

Dank - Pronounced as "dank"

Meaning: High-quality or excellent.

Usage: "These memes are so dank."

Dope - Pronounced as "dohp"

Meaning: Cool or excellent.

Usage: "That new song is dope!"

DR - Pronounced as "dee-ahr"

Meaning: Abbreviation for "Designated Driver."

Usage: "I'll be the DD tonight."

Dubs - Pronounced as "duhbz"

Meaning: Wheels or rims on a car.

Usage: "He's got dubs on his ride."

DTR - Pronounced as "dee-tee-ar"

Meaning: Abbreviation for "Define the Relationship."

Usage: "We need to have a DTR talk."

Doxxing - Pronounced as "doks-ing"

Meaning: Searching for and publishing private information about someone online.

Usage: "He got in trouble for doxxing his ex."

Dummy - Pronounced as "duh-mee"

Meaning: Foolish or stupid.

Usage: "Don't be a dummy."

Deadass - Pronounced as "ded-ass"

Meaning: To be serious or truthful.

Usage: "I'm deadass about this."

Dead - Pronounced as "ded"

Meaning: Something boring or without life.

Usage: "The party was dead."

Dime - Pronounced as "dahym"

Meaning: A perfect ten or an attractive person.

Usage: "She's a dime."

Dead - Pronounced as "ded"

Meaning: Something boring or without life.

Usage: "The party was dead."

Dank - Pronounced as "dank"

Meaning: High-quality or excellent.

Usage: "These memes are so dank."

Drippin' - Pronounced as "drih-pin"

Meaning: Wearing fashionable or stylish clothing.

Usage: "She's drippin' with that outfit."

Dope - Pronounced as "dohp"

Meaning: Cool or excellent.

Usage: "That new song is dope!"

Down - Pronounced as "doun"

Meaning: Being supportive or in agreement with something.

Usage: "I'm down for pizza tonight."

Dusted - Pronounced as "duhs-ted"

Meaning: Being high or intoxicated.

Usage: "He's totally dusted after the party."

Drama llama - Pronounced as "drah-mah lah-muh"

Meaning: Someone who is involved in or attracts drama.

Usage: "She's such a drama llama."

Dank - Pronounced as "dank"

Meaning: High-quality or excellent.

Usage: "These memes are so dank."

Dank - Pronounced as "dank"

Meaning: High-quality or excellent.

Usage: "These memes are so dank."

Dumb - Pronounced as "duhm"

Meaning: Stupid or foolish.

Usage: "That was a dumb move."

Duck - Pronounced as "duhk"

Meaning: To avoid or dodge something.

Usage: "I need to duck that drama."

Dono - Pronounced as "doh-noh"

Meaning: Abbreviation for "I don't know."

Usage: "Dono what to do about it."

Dank - Pronounced as "dank"

Meaning: High-quality or excellent.

Usage: "These memes are so dank."

Devo - Pronounced as "dee-voh"

Meaning: Short for "devastated," expressing extreme disappointment.

Usage: "I'm so devo that I missed the concert."

Dad joke - Pronounced as "dad johk"

Meaning: A pun or joke perceived as uncool or cheesy, often made by dads.

Usage: "That was such a dad joke."

Dead - Pronounced as "ded"

Meaning: Something boring or without life.

Usage: "The party was dead."

Double down - Pronounced as "duhb-uhl doun"

Meaning: To reinforce or emphasize a statement or action.

Usage: "He's doubling down on his argument."

Drop - Pronounced as "drop"

Meaning: Releasing or launching something.

Usage: "They're gonna drop their new album soon."

Duckface - Pronounced as "duhk-feys"

Meaning: Posing for a selfie by puckering lips like a duck.

Usage: "Stop making a duckface in every picture."

Downvote - Pronounced as "doun-vōt"

Meaning: Indicating disapproval or voting negatively on online content.

Usage: "I'll have to downvote that post."

Disco nap - Pronounced as "dis-koh nap"

Meaning: A short sleep or nap before going out at night.

Usage: "I need a disco nap before the party."

Doxxing - Pronounced as "doks-ing"

Meaning: Searching for and publishing private information about someone online.

Usage: "He got in trouble for doxxing his ex."

Dope - Pronounced as "dohp"

Meaning: Cool or excellent.

Usage: "That new song is dope!"

Dabbing - Pronounced as "dab-ing"

Meaning: A dance move where a person raises an arm and tucks their face into the elbow while extending the other arm.

Usage: "He's dabbing in every photo."

Dig - Pronounced as "dig"

Meaning: To like or appreciate something.

Usage: "I dig your style."

Darty - Pronounced as "dahr-tee"

Meaning: A daytime party.

Usage: "Let's hit that darty this weekend."

Drank - Pronounced as "drangk"

Meaning: Alcoholic beverages, especially when referring to lean or purple drank.

Usage: "They're sipping on that drank."

Dubs - Pronounced as "duhbz"

Meaning: Wheels or rims on a car.

Usage: "He's got dubs on his ride."

Dime - Pronounced as "dahym"

Meaning: A perfect ten or an attractive person.

Usage: "She's a dime."

Down for the count - Pronounced as "doun fawr thuh kownt"

Meaning: Being completely defeated or incapacitated.

Usage: "After that workout, I'm down for the count."

Dingus - Pronounced as "ding-uhs"

Meaning: A foolish or idiotic person.

Usage: "Stop acting like a dingus."

E

Extra - Pronounced as "ek-struh"

> ***Meaning:*** Overly dramatic or exaggerated.

> ***Usage:*** "She's so extra about everything."

Epic fail - Pronounced as "ep-ik feyl"

> ***Meaning:*** A huge or significant failure.

> ***Usage:*** "That exam was an epic fail."

Esskeetit - Pronounced as "es-kuh-teet"

> ***Meaning:*** To express excitement or enthusiasm.

> ***Usage:*** "Let's go, esskeetit!"

E-girl/E-boy - Pronounced as "ee-gurl" / "ee-boy"

> ***Meaning:*** Internet personas characterized by certain fashion and behavior styles.

> ***Usage:*** "She's totally into the E-girl aesthetic."

Endgame - Pronounced as "end-geym"

> ***Meaning:*** The final or ultimate stage or outcome.

Usage: "This project is the endgame for us."

Easter egg - Pronounced as "ees-ter eg"

Meaning: A hidden or secret feature or detail, especially in games or software.

Usage: "Did you find that Easter egg in the game?"

Elevenses - Pronounced as "el-uh-vuhn-siz"

Meaning: A snack or meal consumed around 11 a.m.

Usage: "I usually have my elevenses at work."

Emoji fam - Pronounced as "ee-moh-jee fam"

Meaning: A group or community of people communicating mostly with emojis.

Usage: "We're an emoji fam in our group chat."

Ex - Pronounced as "eks"

Meaning: A former romantic partner.

Usage: "I'm meeting my ex for coffee."

Eco-friendly - Pronounced as "eeko frend-lee"

Meaning: Being environmentally conscious or sustainable.

Usage: "I try to use eco-friendly products."

Edgy - Pronounced as "ej-ee"

Meaning: Having a bold or unconventional style or attitude.

Usage: "His clothing style is so edgy."

Eggplant emoji - Pronounced as "eg-plant ee-moh-jee"

Meaning: A symbol often used to represent male genitalia, especially in sexting or suggestive contexts.

Usage: "He sent me the eggplant emoji."

Extracurricular - Pronounced as "ek-struh-kuh-rik-yuh-ler"

Meaning: Activities pursued outside of regular academic courses.

Usage: "I'm involved in many extracurriculars."

Expo - Pronounced as "eks-poh"

>**Meaning:** An event or exhibition.

>**Usage:** "We're attending the tech expo next week."

Ergonomic - Pronounced as "ur-guh-nom-ik"

>**Meaning:** Designed for efficiency and comfort in a working environment.

>**Usage:** "My new chair is so ergonomic."

Eavesdrop - Pronounced as "eavz-drop"

>**Meaning:** Secretly listening to a conversation.

>**Usage:** "I accidentally eavesdropped on their conversation."

Eve - Pronounced as "eev"

>**Meaning:** The day or evening before an event.

>**Usage:** "I'll see you at the party eve."

Excelsior - Pronounced as "ek-sel-see-er"

>**Meaning:** An expression used to convey determination or enthusiasm.

>**Usage:** "Excelsior, let's ace this!"

Eclipse - Pronounced as "ee-klips"

> *Meaning:* To surpass or overshadow someone or something.

> *Usage:* "Her talent eclipses all others."

Elicit - Pronounced as "i-lis-it"

> *Meaning:* To evoke or draw out a reaction or response.

> *Usage:* "His speech elicited applause."

Essential - Pronounced as "uh-sen-shuhl"

> *Meaning:* Extremely important or necessary.

> *Usage:* "Water is essential for life."

Epidemic - Pronounced as "ep-uh-dem-ik"

> *Meaning:* A widespread occurrence of an infectious disease.

> *Usage:* "The flu has reached epidemic levels."

Equinox - Pronounced as "ee-kwuh-noks"

> *Meaning:* The time when day and night are of equal length.

> *Usage:* "The equinox marks the beginning of spring."

Entourage - Pronounced as "ahn-tuh-rahzh"

> *Meaning:* A group of companions or supporters.

> *Usage:* "He arrived with his entourage."

Enigma - Pronounced as "uh-nig-muh"

> *Meaning:* Something mysterious or puzzling.

> *Usage:* "Her behavior is an enigma."

Elitist - Pronounced as "ee-lee-tist"

> *Meaning:* Someone who believes they are superior or exclusive based on their social status or achievements.

> *Usage:* "He comes off as an elitist because of his comments."

Elixir - Pronounced as "ih-liks-er"

> *Meaning:* A magical or medicinal potion, often used humorously.

> *Usage:* "Coffee is my morning elixir."

Ecto - Pronounced as "ek-toh"

> *Meaning:* Excellent or cool, often referencing something ghostly or nostalgic.

> *Usage:* "That retro video game console is ecto!"

E-Boy/E-Girl - Pronounced as "ee-boy" / "ee-girl"

> *Meaning:* Internet personas characterized by certain fashion and behavior styles.

> *Usage:* "He's into the E-boy aesthetic."

Edge - Pronounced as "ej"

> *Meaning:* Being slightly aggressive or intense.

> *Usage:* "His personality has an edgy vibe."

En Pointe - Pronounced as "ahn pwent"

> ***Meaning:*** In a position of perfect balance or alignment, often used in ballet terminology.

> ***Usage:*** "Her performance was en pointe."

Etch - Pronounced as "ech"

> ***Meaning:*** To leave a lasting impression or mark on something.

> ***Usage:*** "Her words etched in my memory."

Ego boost - Pronounced as "ee-goh boost"

> ***Meaning:*** A confidence or self-esteem increase.

> ***Usage:*** "Getting compliments is such an ego boost."

Eureka - Pronounced as "yoo-ree-kuh"

> ***Meaning:*** An exclamation used to express a sudden discovery or realization.

> ***Usage:*** "Eureka! I found the solution."

Euphoria - Pronounced as "yoo-fohr-ee-uh"

> ***Meaning:*** A feeling of extreme happiness or pleasure.

Usage: "Winning the championship brought euphoria."

Edge lord - Pronounced as "ej lord"

Meaning: Someone who enjoys pushing boundaries or being controversial, often for attention.

Usage: "He's such an edge lord on social media."

Ease up - Pronounced as "eez uhhp"

Meaning: To relax or take it easy.

Usage: "You need to ease up and unwind."

Eloquence - Pronounced as "ehl-uh-kwuhns"

Meaning: The art of speaking or writing gracefully and persuasively.

Usage: "Her eloquence captivated the audience."

Exponential - Pronounced as "ek-spuh-nen-shuhl"

Meaning: Growing or increasing rapidly.

Usage: "The popularity of the app grew exponentially."

F

Flex - Pronounced as "fleks"

Meaning: To show off or boast about something.
Usage: "He loves to flex his new car."

Fam - Pronounced as "fam"

Meaning: Close friends or family.

Usage: "Chilling with the fam this weekend."

Finsta - Pronounced as "fin-stuh"

Meaning: A fake or secondary Instagram account used for private or humorous posts.

Usage: "Follow my finsta for silly updates."

Fire - Pronounced as "fai-er"

Meaning: Exceptional, excellent, or exciting.

Usage: "That song is straight fire!"

FOMO - Pronounced as "foh-moh"

Meaning: Fear of missing out, the anxiety of not being present for something exciting or interesting.

Usage: "I have serious FOMO about not going to the concert."

Fleek - Pronounced as "fleek"

Meaning: On point or perfectly styled.

Usage: "Her makeup is on fleek."

Finesse - Pronounced as "fi-ness"

Meaning: To handle skillfully or smoothly.

Usage: "He managed to finesse his way into the party."

Fr - Pronounced as "eff-ahr"

Meaning: Abbreviation for "for real."

Usage: "Are you fr right now?"

FTW - Pronounced as "eff-tee-dubl-yoo"

Meaning: Abbreviation for "For The Win."

Usage: "Pizza FTW!"

Frontin' - Pronounced as "fruhn-tin"

Meaning: Pretending or putting up a false appearance. *Usage:* "Stop frontin' and be yourself."

Flexitarian - Pronounced as "flek-si-tair-ee-uhn"
Meaning: A person who primarily follows a vegetarian diet but occasionally eats meat.

Usage: "She's a flexitarian, mostly veggie but sometimes eats meat."

Finna - Pronounced as "fin-uh"

Meaning: A contraction of "fixing to" or "going to." *Usage:* "I'm finna head out soon."

Fo'shizzle - Pronounced as "foh-shiz-zuhl"

Meaning: An enthusiastic affirmation, slang made famous by Snoop Dogg.

Usage: "Fo'shizzle, that's what I'm talking about!"

Faded - Pronounced as "fey-did"

Meaning: Intoxicated or high, often due to alcohol or drugs.

Usage: "He was so faded at the party."

Frap - Pronounced as "frap"

Meaning: A blend of "friend" and "rap," referring to a friendly conversation.

Usage: "We had a good frap last night."

Facepalm - Pronounced as "feys-pahm"

Meaning: A gesture or expression of disbelief or frustration.

Usage: "*Facepalm* I can't believe I forgot."

Fleeky - Pronounced as "flee-kee"

Meaning: Looking exceptionally good or stylish.

Usage: "Her outfit is so fleeky today."

Freestyle - Pronounced as "free-stahyl"

Meaning: Improvised or spontaneous performance, often in music or rap.

Usage: "He dropped a sick freestyle at the party."

Fizzled - Pronounced as "fiz-uhld"

Meaning: When a plan or situation fails or falls apart.

Usage: "The party fizzled out early."

Foolery - Pronounced as "foo-luh-ree"

Meaning: Nonsense or foolish behavior.

Usage: "Stop with the foolery and focus."

Fasho - Pronounced as "fah-shoh"

Meaning: An affirmation or agreement, short for "for sure."

Usage: "Want to grab some lunch? Fasho!"

Fubbing - Pronounced as "fuhb-ing"

Meaning: Ignoring someone in favor of paying attention to a phone or mobile device.

Usage: "She's always fubbing people during conversations."

Fuego - Pronounced as "fwey-goh"

Meaning: Hot or excellent, often used to describe music or food.

Usage: "This track is fuego!"

Flewed out - Pronounced as "floo-d out"

Meaning: To go somewhere, often with an implication of luxury or expense.

Usage: "She flewed out to Paris for the weekend."

Fro-yo - Pronounced as "froh-yoh"

Meaning: Frozen yogurt, a popular dessert.

Usage: "Let's get some fro-yo after dinner."

Festie - Pronounced as "fes-tee"

Meaning: Someone who loves attending festivals or events.

Usage: "She's a total festie, always at music festivals."

Finest - Pronounced as "fai-nist"

Meaning: The best or most attractive.

Usage: "He's the finest guy in the room."

Flame - Pronounced as "fleym"

Meaning: To insult or criticize someone harshly.

Usage: "He flamed his friend's outfit."

Flop - Pronounced as "flop"

Meaning: A complete failure or disaster.

Usage: "The movie was a total flop."

G

Gucci - Pronounced as "goo-chee"

Meaning: Good or cool, derived from the luxury fashion brand.

Usage: "Everything's Gucci, no worries."

Ghost - Pronounced as "gohst"

Meaning: To disappear or stop communicating abruptly. *Usage:* "He ghosted me after our date."

GOAT - Pronounced as "goht"

Meaning: Acronym for "Greatest of All Time."

Usage: "She's the GOAT in her field."

Grind - Pronounced as "grahynd"

Meaning: Working hard or hustling towards a goal.

Usage: "I've been on the grind all week."

Goals - Pronounced as "gohls"

Meaning: Used to express admiration or inspiration.

Usage: "Their relationship is goals."

Gassed - Pronounced as "gast"

Meaning: Overly excited or hyped up about something. *Usage:* "He's gassed about the concert."

Gig - Pronounced as "gig"

Meaning: A job or assignment, especially in the gig economy.

Usage: "She got a gig as a freelance writer."

Glow up - Pronounced as "gloh uhp"

Meaning: A transformation, often personal or physical, resulting in an improvement.

Usage: "Her glow up after high school was amazing."

G - Pronounced as "jee"

Meaning: Short for "gangster" or "gangsta," used to refer to friends or associates.

Usage: "What's up, G?"

Get lit - Pronounced as "get lit"

Meaning: To have an exciting or fun time.

Usage: "Let's get lit at the party tonight!"

Grub - Pronounced as "gruhb"

Meaning: Food or a meal.

Usage: "Let's grab some grub before the movie."

Genius - Pronounced as "jee-nee-uhs"

Meaning: Used sarcastically to describe a foolish or ridiculous action.

Usage: "That's a genius idea, not!"

Glitch - Pronounced as "glitch"

Meaning: A malfunction or unexpected problem, especially in technology.

Usage: "There's a glitch in the system."

Gnarly - Pronounced as "nar-lee"

Meaning: Extreme or intense, often used to describe something cool or impressive.

Usage: "That skateboard trick was gnarly!"

Giddy - Pronounced as "gid-ee"

Meaning: Excited or thrilled about something.

Usage: "I'm feeling giddy about the concert."

Gaslight - Pronounced as "gas-lahyt"

Meaning: To manipulate or deceive someone into questioning their own sanity.

Usage: "He's trying to gaslight her about the argument."

H

High-key - Pronounced as "hahy-kee"

Meaning: Used to emphasize something that is openly known or expressed.

Usage: "I'm high-key excited for the concert tonight!"

Hundo P - Pronounced as "huhn-doh pee"

Meaning: Short for "hundred percent," expressing complete agreement or certainty.

Usage: "That's hundo P the best pizza in town!"

Hangry - Pronounced as "hang-gree"

Meaning: A combination of hungry and angry, describing irritability due to hunger.

Usage: "I get hangry if I skip meals."

Hype - Pronounced as "hahyp"

Meaning: To promote or create excitement about something.

Usage: "The new game release is getting a lot of hype."

Haterade - Pronounced as "hey-tuh-reyd"

Meaning: Negative attitudes or behavior towards someone or something.

Usage: "She's been drinking haterade lately."

Hit me up - Pronounced as "hit mee uhp"

Meaning: Ask someone to contact or message you.

Usage: "If you need anything, hit me up."

Hundo - Pronounced as "huhn-doh"

Meaning: Short for "hundred," indicating complete agreement or certainty.

Usage: "I'm a hundo percent sure about this."

Haul - Pronounced as "hawl"

Meaning: A collection of recently purchased items, often showcased online.

Usage: "Check out my makeup haul!"

Hecka - Pronounced as "hek-uh"

Meaning: An emphasis on "very" or "a lot."

Usage: "That's hecka cool!"

Headass - Pronounced as "hed-as"

Meaning: Used to describe someone who's acting foolish or naive.

Usage: "Stop being a headass!"

Hot take - Pronounced as "haht teyk"

Meaning: A controversial or unconventional opinion.

Usage: "That's a hot take on the new movie."

I

Ish - Pronounced as "ish"

Meaning: A suffix indicating something approximate or vague.

Usage: "The movie starts at 7-ish."

Ight - Pronounced as "ahyt"

Meaning: Short for "alright."

Usage: "I'll see you later, ight?"

I'm dead - Pronounced as "ahym ded" *Meaning:* Used to express extreme amusement or shock. *Usage:* "His joke was so funny, I'm dead!"

IDK - Pronounced as "ahy-dee-kay"

Meaning: Abbreviation for "I don't know."

Usage: "IDK where my phone is."

IRL - Pronounced as "eye-ahr-el"

Meaning: Abbreviation for "In Real Life."

Usage: "We finally met IRL."

It's a vibe - Pronounced as "its uh vahyb"

Meaning: Refers to a situation or experience that has a good atmosphere or feeling.

Usage: "This party is a vibe tonight!"

In the feels - Pronounced as "in the feels"

Meaning: When something deeply affects emotions, often referring to a sentimental moment.

Usage: "That movie got me in the feels."

Iffy - Pronounced as "if-ee"

Meaning: Uncertain or doubtful.

Usage: "The weather forecast for tomorrow is iffy."

Ice - Pronounced as "ahys"

Meaning: Diamonds or jewelry, often used in hip-hop culture.

Usage: "He's got ice all over him."

Imma - Pronounced as "im-uh"

Meaning: Short for "I'm going to" or "I will."

Usage: "Imma head to the gym after work."

Ikr - Pronounced as "eye-kay-ahr"

Meaning: Abbreviation for "I know, right?"

Usage: "That movie was terrible, IKR?"

ICYMI - Pronounced as "ahy-see-em-ayy"

Meaning: Abbreviation for "In Case You Missed It."

Usage: "ICYMI, they announced the new schedule yesterday."

IMHO - Pronounced as "eye-em-aych-oh"

Meaning: Abbreviation for "In My Humble Opinion."

Usage: "IMHO, that restaurant has the best burgers."

I'm shook - Pronounced as "ahym shook"

Meaning: Feeling shocked or surprised.

Usage: "I'm shook after watching that scary movie."

Iconic - Pronounced as "ahy-kon-ik"

Meaning: Something or someone widely recognized and admired.

Usage: "That performance was iconic!"

J

JOMO - Pronounced as "joh-moh"

Meaning: Joy of Missing Out, indicating contentment with staying in or avoiding social events.

Usage: "I prefer JOMO over going out sometimes."

Juice - Pronounced as "joos"

Meaning: Influence or power.

Usage: "He's got a lot of juice in that industry."

Jawn - Pronounced as "jawn"

Meaning: A term used to describe a person, place, or thing (Philadelphia slang).

Usage: "That's a cool jawn you got there."

Janky - Pronounced as "jan-kee"

Meaning: Of poor or questionable quality.

Usage: "The Wi-Fi here is so janky."

Jelly - Pronounced as "jel-ee"

Meaning: Jealous.

Usage: "She's totally jelly of her friend's success."

Just saying - Pronounced as "just say-ing"

Meaning: Used before or after making a point, often to soften a statement.

Usage: "She's always late, just saying."

JSYK - Pronounced as "juh-sik"

Meaning: Abbreviation for "Just so you know."

Usage: "JSYK, the party starts at 9."

K

Kickback - Pronounced as "kik-bak"

Meaning: A casual get-together or small party.

Usage: "We're having a kickback at my place tonight."

Key - Pronounced as "kee"

Meaning: Important or crucial.

Usage: "Sleep is key for a healthy lifestyle."

Keep it 100 - Pronounced as "keep it one hundred"

Meaning: To be genuine or honest.

Usage: "I always keep it 100 with my friends."

Kewl - Pronounced as "kewl"

Meaning: A variant spelling of "cool."

Usage: "That's so kewl!"

K - Pronounced as "kay"

Meaning: Okay or understood.

Usage: "K, see you later!"

Kicks - Pronounced as "kiks"

Meaning: Sneakers or shoes.

Usage: "Check out my new kicks!"

Karen - Pronounced as "kar-en"

Meaning: A pejorative term used for an entitled or demanding middle-aged woman.

Usage: "She's being a total Karen right now."

Killin' it - Pronounced as "kil-in it"

Meaning: Doing exceptionally well.

Usage: "She's killin' it in her new job."

Kudos - Pronounced as "koo-dohs"

Meaning: Praise or congratulations.

Usage: "Kudos on acing the exam!"

L

Lit - Pronounced as "lit"

Meaning: Amazing, exciting, or awesome.

Usage: "The party last night was so lit!"

Low-key - Pronounced as "loh-kee"

Meaning: To keep something quiet or secretive, or to express something in a subtle way.

Usage: "I'm low-key into that new TV show."

LOL - Pronounced as "el-oh-el"

Meaning: Abbreviation for "Laugh out loud."

Usage: "That meme was hilarious, LOL!"

Legit - Pronounced as "lee-jit"

Meaning: Real, genuine, or authentic.

Usage: "Her skills are legit."

Lurk - Pronounced as "lurk"

Meaning: To quietly observe someone's social media profile without engaging or interacting.

Usage: "I'm just going to lurk on their Instagram for a bit."

Let's go - Pronounced as "lets goh"

Meaning: Expressing excitement or agreement.

Usage: "You aced the test? Let's go!"

Flex - Pronounced as "fleks"

Meaning: To show off or boast about something.

Usage: "He loves to flex his new car."

Litty - Pronounced as "lit-ee"

Meaning: Extremely exciting or enjoyable.

Usage: "The concert last night was litty!"

Lost in the sauce - Pronounced as "lost in thuh saws"

Meaning: Confused or disoriented.

Usage: "I'm completely lost in the sauce with this math problem."

Lame - Pronounced as "leym"

Meaning: Uncool or boring.

Usage: "That party was so lame."

Lamestream - Pronounced as "leym-streem"

Meaning: Refers to mainstream media or ideas perceived as uninteresting or outdated.

Usage: "I'm tired of the lamestream news."

Legend - Pronounced as "leh-jend"

Meaning: Someone admired or respected for their actions or character.

Usage: "He's a legend in the gaming community."

Lurker - Pronounced as "lur-kuhr"

Meaning: Someone who quietly observes but doesn't engage in online discussions or activities,

Usage: "She's a lurker on forums."

LFG - Pronounced as "el-eff-gee"

Meaning: Abbreviation for "Let's freaking go!"

Usage: "LFG, it's time for the concert!"

Lezzgo - Pronounced as "lez-goh"

Meaning: Let's go or expressing excitement.

Usage: "Lezzgo hit the gym!"

Lush - Pronounced as "luhsh"

Meaning: Describing something as attractive, pleasant, or enjoyable.

Usage: "That party was lush."

Linkup - Pronounced as "link-uhp"

Meaning: Getting together or meeting up with friends.

Usage: "We should plan a linkup this weekend."

Live - Pronounced as "liv"

Meaning: Exciting or enjoyable.

Usage: "The concert was so live!"

Lifestyle - Pronounced as "lahyf-stahyl"

Meaning: A particular way of living or the things a person enjoys doing.

Usage: "She's all about that healthy lifestyle."

Lick - Pronounced as "lik"

Meaning: To steal or obtain something easily.

Usage: "He got that job like a lick."

Lit AF - Pronounced as "lit ey-eff"

Meaning: Extremely exciting or enjoyable, often emphasized with "AF" meaning "as heck" or "as f*."

Usage: "The party last night was lit AF!"

Low-key high-key - Pronounced as "loh-kee hahy-kee"

Meaning: To express something subtly (low-key) and explicitly (high-key) at the same time.

Usage: "I'm low-key high-key excited about this weekend."

M

Mood - Pronounced as "moohd"

Meaning: Used to express agreement or resonance with something.

Usage: "Watching movies all day? Mood."

Mint - Pronounced as "mint"

Meaning: Something that is excellent, great, or in perfect condition.

Usage: "Your outfit looks mint!"

Mukbang - Pronounced as "muk-bang"

Meaning: A live online audiovisual broadcast featuring a host eating large quantities of food while interacting with their audience.

Usage: "Have you seen that mukbang stream?"

Munted - Pronounced as "mun-ted"

Meaning: Extremely intoxicated or under the influence of drugs.

Usage: "He got completely munted at the party."

Mood AF - Pronounced as "moohd ey-eff"

Meaning: Emphasizing a feeling or situation strongly.

Usage: "Exams tomorrow? Mood AF."

Mugged Off - Pronounced as "muhgd awf"

Meaning: To be treated unfairly or disrespected.

Usage: "I got totally mugged off by my boss."

Meltdown - Pronounced as "mel-doun"

Meaning: A moment of emotional distress or breakdown.

Usage: "She had a meltdown after losing her phone."

Murked - Pronounced as "murkt"

Meaning: Defeated decisively, embarrassed, or outsmarted.

Usage: "He got murked in the debate."

Mystery Box - Pronounced as "mis-tuh-ree boks"

Meaning: A surprise package, often purchased without knowing its contents.

Usage: "I ordered a mystery box from that online store."

Megxit - Pronounced as "megz-it"

Meaning: The departure of Meghan Markle and Prince Harry from the British royal family.

Usage: "The media covered Megxit extensively."

Muffin top - Pronounced as "muhf-in top"

Meaning: When someone's midsection hangs over the waistband of their pants, resembling the top of a muffin.

Usage: "I need to hit the gym; I'm getting a muffin top."

Mega - Pronounced as "meh-gah"

Meaning: Extremely large, significant, or impressive.

Usage: "That concert was mega!"

Mukka - Pronounced as "muh-kuh"

Meaning: A close friend or buddy.

Usage: "He's my mukka from school."

Mum bod - Pronounced as "muhm bod"

Meaning: A body shape characterized by having had children, often in a positive and empowering way.

Usage: "She's confident and embracing her mum bod."

McMansion - Pronounced as "mik-man-shuhn"

Meaning: A large, ostentatious house, typically lacking in architectural integrity.

Usage: "That new neighborhood is full of McMansions."

Meme-worthy - Pronounced as "meem-wur-thee"

Meaning: Describing something or someone that's suitable or likely to become a popular meme.

Usage: "That facial expression is totally meme-worthy."

Meep - Pronounced as "meep"

Meaning: An expression used to acknowledge a small mistake or accident.

Usage: "Oops, I dropped my phone... meep."

Minted - Pronounced as "min-tid"

Meaning: To be extremely wealthy or rich.

Usage: "She's absolutely minted with her new business."

Monet - Pronounced as "moh-ney"

Meaning: Someone or something that looks good from a distance but not up close.

Usage: "Her room is a bit of a Monet."

Muppet - Pronounced as "muhp-it"

Meaning: Used to describe someone as foolish or silly.

Usage: "Stop acting like a muppet!"

Mula - Pronounced as "myoo-luh"

Meaning: Money or cash.

Usage: "I need some extra mula for the concert tickets."

Mum bod - Pronounced as "muhm bod"

Meaning: A body shape characterized by having had children, often in a positive and empowering way.

Usage: "She's confident and embracing her mum bod."

N

No cap - Pronounced as "no kap"

Meaning: To speak the truth or express sincerity, often used to emphasize a statement.

Usage: "That party was amazing, no cap!"

NGL - Pronounced as "en-jee-el"

Meaning: Abbreviation for "Not gonna lie."

Usage: "NGL, I'm really excited for the new album."

Noms - Pronounced as "nahms"

Meaning: Delicious food or a meal.

Usage: "I'm craving some noms right now."

Nood - Pronounced as "nood"

Meaning: A casual or relaxed state.

Usage: "I'm in a total nood mood today."

Natch - Pronounced as "nach"

Meaning: Naturally or of course.

Usage: "Of course, I'll be there, natch!"

Nae Nae - Pronounced as "ney ney"

Meaning: A popular dance move.

Usage: "He did the Nae Nae at the party."

NBD - Pronounced as "en-bee-dee"

Meaning: Abbreviation for "No Big Deal."

Usage: "Missed the bus, but it's NBD."

Narked - Pronounced as "nahrkt"

Meaning: Annoyed or irritated.

Usage: "She got narked when he canceled the plans."

Netizen - Pronounced as "net-i-zen"

Meaning: An active user or participant in online communities or on the internet.

Usage: "He's a famous netizen on social media."

Newb - Pronounced as "noo-b"

Meaning: A newcomer or someone inexperienced in a particular activity.

Usage: "He's such a newb at gaming."

Nays - Pronounced as "nayz"

Meaning: Negative or adverse opinions.

Usage: "Ignore the nays; pursue your dreams!"

Netflix and chill - Pronounced as "net-flks and chil"

Meaning: To watch Netflix together or hang out in a relaxed setting, often implying romantic intentions.

Usage: "We just Netflix and chill at home."

Nagl - Pronounced as "nah-guhl"

Meaning: Abbreviation for "Not a good look."

Usage: "Wearing socks with sandals is nagl."

Nonce - Pronounced as "nons"

Meaning: A person who is considered strange or odd.

Usage: "He's a bit of a nonce."

Nudge - Pronounced as "nuhj"

Meaning: To gently remind or draw attention to something.

Usage: "Can you nudge me when it's time to leave?"

Neckbeard - Pronounced as "nek-beerd"

Meaning: An insulting term for someone who is socially inept, often used online.

Usage: "He's a typical neckbeard."

NIFOC - Pronounced as "neye-fok"

Meaning: Abbreviation for "Naked In Front Of Computer."

Usage: "Caught him being NIFOC late at night."

Nosh - Pronounced as "nahsh"

Meaning: Food or a meal, especially when eaten enthusiastically.

Usage: "I had a great nosh at the new restaurant."

Nutter - Pronounced as "nuht-er"

Meaning: A crazy or eccentric person.

Usage: "He's a bit of a nutter sometimes."

Nooky - Pronounced as "nuh-kee"

Meaning: Sex or intimate activities.

Usage: "They went for a bit of nooky last night."

Noob - Pronounced as "noob"

Meaning: A newcomer or someone inexperienced in a particular activity.

Usage: "She's a total noob at playing guitar."

Nudge - Pronounced as "nuhj"

Meaning: To gently remind or draw attention to something.

Usage: "Can you nudge me when it's time to leave?"

O

OG - Pronounced as "oh-jee"

> *Meaning:* Stands for "Original Gangster" or someone with experience or authenticity.

> *Usage:* "He's an OG in the skateboarding scene."

On fleek - Pronounced as "on fleek"

> *Meaning:* Looking perfectly styled or on point.

> *Usage:* "Her makeup is on fleek today!"

OMG - Pronounced as "oh-em-gee"

> *Meaning:* Abbreviation for "Oh my God!"

> *Usage:* "OMG, did you see that?"

OTP - Pronounced as "oh-tee-pee"

> *Meaning:* Abbreviation for "One True Pairing," referring to a favorite romantic couple.

> *Usage:* "They're my OTP in that TV show."

Oof - Pronounced as "oof"

> *Meaning:* An expression used when something is disappointing or painful.

Usage: "I forgot my wallet at home... oof."

Outta pocket - Pronounced as "ow-tuh pok-it"

Meaning: Behaving inappropriately or saying something offensive.

Usage: "His comments were outta pocket."

Overshare - Pronounced as "oh-ver-sheyr"

Meaning: To give too much personal information.

Usage: "She tends to overshare on social media."

Over it - Pronounced as "oh-ver it"

Meaning: Fed up or no longer interested in something.

Usage: "I'm so over this drama."

Off the hook - Pronounced as "awf thuh huk"

Meaning: Free from obligation or no longer in trouble.

Usage: "Luckily, I got off the hook for the mistake."

Off the chain - Pronounced as "awf thuh cheyn"

Meaning: Exceptional or extraordinary.

Usage: "That party was off the chain!"

Op - Pronounced as "op"

Meaning: Short for "opposite" or "opponent."

Usage: "They're the op team in the game."

On point - Pronounced as "on point"

Meaning: Something that is well-executed or perfectly done.

Usage: "Your outfit is on point!"

Overrated - Pronounced as "oh-ver-ray-ted"

Meaning: Something or someone given more credit than deserved.

Usage: "That movie was overrated."

Overachiever - Pronounced as "oh-ver-uh-chee-vur"

Meaning: Someone who excels or performs beyond expectations.

Usage: "She's such an overachiever in school."

Overseas - Pronounced as "oh-ver-sees"

Meaning: Abroad or in another country.

Usage: "I'm traveling overseas next month."

Owe - Pronounced as "oh"

Meaning: Short for "own" or to acknowledge.

Usage: "I owe you an apology."

Out of the loop - Pronounced as "owt uhv thuh loop"

Meaning: Not informed or unaware of current events or information.

Usage: "I feel out of the loop with the latest trends."

Own it - Pronounced as "ohn it"

Meaning: To confidently accept or take responsibility for something.

Usage: "Just own it and move forward."

Out of sight - Pronounced as "owt uhv sahyt"

Meaning: Remarkable or fantastic.

Usage: "That party was out of sight!"

Outdoorsy - Pronounced as "owt-dawr-zee"

Meaning: Someone who enjoys spending time outside or participating in outdoor activities.

Usage: "She's very outdoorsy and loves hiking."

Obvi - Pronounced as "ob-vee"

Meaning: Short for "obviously."

Usage: "Obvi, I'll be there on time."

Oversleep - Pronounced as "oh-ver-sleep"

Meaning: To sleep longer than intended or miss an alarm.

Usage: "I overslept and missed the meeting."

On the reg - Pronounced as "on thuh rej"

Meaning: Regularly or frequently.

Usage: "I work out on the reg."

Off-brand - Pronounced as "awf-brand"

Meaning: Not the original or not as well-known.

Usage: "That's an off-brand version of the product."

Omnishambles - Pronounced as "om-nee-sham-buhlz"

Meaning: A situation characterized by a series of chaotic events.

Usage: "The meeting turned into an omnishambles."

One-hit wonder - Pronounced as "wun-hit wuhn-der"

Meaning: A person or thing that succeeds once but doesn't replicate that success.

Usage: "That band was a one-hit wonder."

Old school - Pronounced as "ohld skool"

Meaning: Something from an earlier era, often referring to something classic or traditional.

Usage: "I like old school hip-hop."

Obvs - Pronounced as "obvs"

Meaning: Short for "obvious."

Usage: "That's obvs the best choice."

Oblivion - Pronounced as "uh-bliv-ee-uhn"

Meaning: A state of being completely unaware or ignored.

Usage: "He disappeared into oblivion after the breakup."

Out of this world - Pronounced as "owt uhv this wurld"

> *Meaning:* Exceptional or extraordinary.
>
> *Usage:* "The dessert was out of this world!"

Over the moon - Pronounced as "oh-ver thuh moon"

> *Meaning:* Extremely happy or delighted.
>
> *Usage:* "She was over the moon with her new job offer." Outdoorsy - Pronounced as "owt-dawr-zee"

Off the chain - Pronounced as "awf thuh cheyn"

> *Meaning:* Exceptional or extraordinary.
>
> *Usage:* "That party was off the chain!"

Outie - Pronounced as "ow-tee"

> *Meaning:* Leaving or heading out.
>
> *Usage:* "I'm outie, see you later."

One-up - Pronounced as "wuhn-uhp"

> *Meaning:* To outdo or surpass someone.
>
> *Usage:* "He always tries to one-up everyone."

On the real - Pronounced as "on thuh reel"

> *Meaning:* To speak honestly or truthfully.

Usage: "I gotta be on the real with you."

On the down low (OTDL) - Pronounced as "on thuh doun loh"

Meaning: Secretly or discreetly.

Usage: "Let's keep this on the down low."

Oh snap - Pronounced as "oh snap"

Meaning: An expression used to show surprise or astonishment.

Usage: "Oh snap, did you see that?"

P

Pandemic chic - Pronounced as "pan-dem-ik sheek"

Meaning: Fashion trends influenced by pandemic lifestyles, such as comfort wear or mask matching.

Usage: "She's rocking pandemic chic with her stylish mask."

Phubbing - Pronounced as "fuhb-ing"

Meaning: Ignoring someone in favor of your phone.

Usage: "Stop phubbing me and pay attention!"

Procrastinasty - Pronounced as "proh-cras-tuh-nas-tee"

Meaning: Procrastinating in an extreme or terrible way.

Usage: "I have a case of procrastinasty."

Pawse - Pronounced as "pawz"

Meaning: A pause induced by someone showing their pet.

Usage: "Sorry for the pawse, but look at my cute dog!"

Pulled an all-nighter - Pronounced as "puld an awl-nahy-ter"

Meaning: Staying awake all night, usually to complete tasks or study.

Usage: "I pulled an all-nighter for the exam."

Pregame - Pronounced as "pree-geym"

Meaning: Drinking alcohol before attending an event or party.

Usage: "Let's pregame before the concert."

Pwned - Pronounced as "pound"

> *Meaning:* To be utterly defeated or outplayed, especially in online gaming.

> *Usage:* "I got pwned in that match."

Peak - Pronounced as "peek"

> *Meaning:* A situation reaching its worst or highest point.

> *Usage:* "Failing the test was the peak of my day."

Perf - Pronounced as "purf"

> *Meaning:* Short for "perfect."

> *Usage:* "Your outfit is perf!"

Plug - Pronounced as "pluhg"

> *Meaning:* A source for something, often drugs but can refer to anything.

> *Usage:* "I know a plug for sneakers."

Ppl - Pronounced as "pee-pee-el"

> *Meaning:* Abbreviation for "people."

> *Usage:* "Ppl loved the new song."

Peep - Pronounced as "peep"

Meaning: To check or look at something or someone.

Usage: "Did you peep that new video?"

Preach - Pronounced as "preech"

Meaning: To strongly agree with something someone said.

Usage: "Preach! That's so true."

Plot twist - Pronounced as "plot twist"

Meaning: A surprising turn of events.

Usage: "That movie had a crazy plot twist."

Posh - Pronounced as "pawsh"

Meaning: Elegant or sophisticated.

Usage: "She looks so posh in that outfit."

Party foul - Pronounced as "pahr-tee fowl"

Meaning: A social mistake or inappropriate behavior at a party.

Usage: "Spilling your drink is a party foul."

Pear - Pronounced as "peer"

Meaning: Short for "pair," often used to express agreement or confirmation.

Usage: "We make a great pear."

Pupperazzi - Pronounced as "puhp-uh-raz-ee"

Meaning: People who take a lot of pictures of their pets.

Usage: "I'm part of the pupperazzi with my dog."

Panic-buying - Pronounced as "pan-ik bahy-ing"

Meaning: Buying large quantities of goods due to fear or uncertainty, often during a crisis.

Usage: "There was panic-buying of toilet paper during the pandemic."

Prolly - Pronounced as "prol-lee"

Meaning: Short for "probably."

Usage: "I'll prolly be there."

Peckish - Pronounced as "pek-ish"

Meaning: Slightly hungry.

Usage: "I'm feeling a bit peckish."

Pawsome - Pronounced as "paw-suhm"

Meaning: Awesome, but with an emphasis on animals or pets.

Usage: "That dog is pawsome!"

Pinky promise - Pronounced as "pink-ee prom-iss"

> **Meaning:** A promise made by intertwining pinky fingers as a sign of sincerity.

> **Usage:** "Let's pinky promise that we'll meet."

Plug and play - Pronounced as "pluhg and plehy"

> **Meaning:** Refers to technology or devices that are easily connected and used.

> **Usage:** "It's a plug-and-play camera."

Pumped - Pronounced as "puhmped"

> **Meaning:** Excited or enthusiastic.

> **Usage:** "I'm pumped for the concert!"

Q

QFT - Pronounced as "kyoo-eff-tee"

Meaning: Stands for "Quoted For Truth," used to express agreement with a quoted statement.

Usage: "QFT, that's exactly how I feel."

Queen - Pronounced as "kween"

Meaning: A term used to praise or acknowledge someone's excellence or authority.

Usage: "She's a true queen at gaming."

Quirky - Pronounced as "kwur-kee"

Meaning: Unusual or eccentric in an interesting way.

Usage: "I love her quirky fashion sense."

Quaran-team - Pronounced as "kwor-an teem"

Meaning: The people with whom you spent time during quarantine.

Usage: "My quaran-team made lockdown bearable."

Que - Pronounced as "kyoo"

Meaning: Abbreviation for "queue," often used in gaming contexts to indicate waiting.

Usage: "Join the que for the next round."

R

Rando - Pronounced as "ran-doh"

Meaning: A random or unknown person.

Usage: "Who's that rando at the party?"

Rekt - Pronounced as "rekt"

Meaning: Completely destroyed or beaten in a game or argument.

Usage: "He got rekt in the match."

Rager - Pronounced as "rey-jer"

Meaning: A wild or crazy party.

Usage: "Last night's party was a rager!"

Rip - Pronounced as "rip"

Meaning: An expression of sympathy or condolences.

Usage: "Rip, that's terrible news."

Rad - Pronounced as "rad"

Meaning: Short for "radical," meaning cool or awesome.

Usage: "That skateboard trick was rad!"

Receipts - Pronounced as "re-seets"

Meaning: Evidence or proof, often used in arguments or discussions.

Usage: "She has the receipts to prove her point."

ROFL - Pronounced as "arr-oh-eff-el"

Meaning: Abbreviation for "Rolling on the floor laughing."

Usage: "That joke had me ROFL!"

Righteous - Pronounced as "rahy-chuhs"

Meaning: Exceptionally good or excellent.

Usage: "This pizza is righteous!"

Run it - Pronounced as "run it"

Meaning: Let's go or let's do it.

Usage: "Ready to run it?"

Roadman - Pronounced as "rohd-man"

Meaning: A person associated with a street or urban lifestyle.

Usage: "He's a proper roadman."

Real talk - Pronounced as "reel tawk"

Meaning: Speaking honestly or seriously.

Usage: "Real talk, we need to sort this out."

Roasted - Pronounced as "roh-sted"

Meaning: Criticized or insulted severely.

Usage: "He got roasted in the debate."

Ride or die - Pronounced as "ryd or dy"

Meaning: Someone loyal and supportive in any situation.

Usage: "She's my ride or die friend."

RBF - Pronounced as "arr-bee-eff"

Meaning: Abbreviation for "Resting B Face," a neutral facial expression that unintentionally appears unfriendly or angry.

Usage: "People often mistake her RBF for being mad."

Respeck - Pronounced as "re-spek"

Meaning: Respect, used to show admiration or appreciation.

Usage: "Put some respeck on his name!"

Return to text - Pronounced as "ri-turn too tekst"

Meaning: Signifying a return to a conversation after being away.

Usage: "Sorry, return to text. What were we saying?"

Re-up - Pronounced as "ree-uhp"

Meaning: To replenish or restock on something.

Usage: "I need to re-up on snacks."

Rock - Pronounced as "rok"

Meaning: To wear or sport an outfit confidently.

Usage: "She's rocking that new dress."

Rawr - Pronounced as "rawr"

Meaning: A playful or exaggerated way to express excitement or anger.

Usage: "Rawr! I can't wait for the concert."

Ripper - Pronounced as "rip-er"

Meaning: A very enjoyable or exciting event.

Usage: "That movie was a ripper!"

Round the way - Pronounced as "rownd thuh wey"

Meaning: In the local area or neighborhood.

Usage: "I grew up round the way."

Rigged - Pronounced as "rigd"

Meaning: When something is unfair or manipulated.

Usage: "The game feels rigged against me."

Recharge - Pronounced as "ree-chahrj"

Meaning: To rest and regain energy.

Usage: "I need to recharge after a long day."

Roomie - Pronounced as "roo-mee"

Meaning: A roommate or housemate.

Usage: "She's my roomie from college."

Rampage - Pronounced as "ram-peyj"

Meaning: Behaving in an uncontrollable or destructive manner.

Usage: "He went on a shopping rampage."

Rec - Pronounced as "rek"

Meaning: To recommend or suggest something.

Usage: "I rec this new TV series."

Regular - Pronounced as "reg-yuh-ler"

Meaning: Something usual or frequent.

Usage: "It's just a regular day."

Ride - Pronounced as "ryd"

Meaning: To support or back someone up.

Usage: "I'll ride for you no matter what."

Razz - Pronounced as "raz"

Meaning: To tease or make fun of someone in a friendly way.

Usage: "He razzes me about my fashion choices."

Relatable - Pronounced as "ree-luh-tuh-buhl"

Meaning: Something that is easy to relate to or understand.

Usage: "That meme is so relatable!"

Remote work - Pronounced as "ri-moht wurk"

Meaning: Working from a location other than the office.

Usage: "I prefer remote work for its flexibility."

Replay - Pronounced as "ree-play"

Meaning: To repeat or rewatch something.

Usage: "I'll have to replay that scene."

Red pill - Pronounced as "red pil"

Meaning: To see or accept a harsh truth or reality.

Usage: "He took the red pill about the situation."

Rope - Pronounced as "rohp"

Meaning: To invite someone to participate in something.

Usage: "Want to rope in for the project?"

Ruffle feathers - Pronounced as "ruhf-uhl fe-thurz"

Meaning: To cause annoyance or irritation.

Usage: "His comments ruffle feathers."

Rain check - Pronounced as "reyn chek"

Meaning: To postpone or reschedule an invitation.

Usage: "Can I take a rain check on dinner?"

Rescue - Pronounced as "re-skew"

Meaning: To help someone out of a difficult situation.

Usage: "She came to my rescue when I needed it."

Real one - Pronounced as "reel wuhn"

Meaning: Someone who is genuine, trustworthy, or loyal.

Usage: "She's a real one; always has my back."

Rudeboy - Pronounced as "rood-boy"

Meaning: Someone tough or rebellious, often used in the context of style or attitude.

Usage: "He's got that rudeboy look."

Risk it for the biscuit - Pronounced as "risk it for thuh bisk-it"

Meaning: Taking a chance or risk for a potential reward.

Usage: "I'll risk it for the biscuit and apply for the job."

S

Salty - Pronounced as "sawl-tee"

Meaning: Being upset or bitter about something.

Usage: "He's feeling salty after losing the game."

Savage - Pronounced as "sav-ij"

Meaning: Acting boldly or ruthlessly without regard for others.

Usage: "She made a savage comeback."

Slay - Pronounced as "sley"

Meaning: To do something exceptionally well or flawlessly.

Usage: "She slays in that outfit!"

Simp - Pronounced as "simp"

Meaning: Someone who goes above and beyond for someone they are interested in, often to an excessive extent.

Usage: "He's simping over her hard."

Shook - Pronounced as "shook"

Meaning: Feeling shocked or surprised.

Usage: "I'm shook by the plot twist."

Stan - Pronounced as "stan"

Meaning: A devoted and enthusiastic fan of a celebrity or brand.

Usage: "She's a huge stan of that singer."

Ship - Pronounced as "ship"

Meaning: To support or endorse a romantic pairing between two individuals.

Usage: "I ship them; they'd make a cute couple."

Sheeple - Pronounced as "shee-puhl"

Meaning: People who follow others without thinking or questioning.

Usage: "They're just sheeple, following trends blindly."

Secure the bag - Pronounced as "si-kyoor thuh bag"

Meaning: To obtain financial success or secure a goal.

Usage: "I'm hustling to secure the bag."

Suss - Pronounced as "suhs"

Meaning: To investigate or figure something out.

Usage: "I need to suss out the situation."

Shade - Pronounced as "sheyd"

Meaning: Disrespectful or insulting behavior towards someone.

Usage: "She threw shade at him during the argument."

Shooketh - Pronounced as "shook-uhth"

Meaning: To be extremely shocked or surprised.

Usage: "I am shooketh by her announcement."

Swag - Pronounced as "swag"

Meaning: A sense of style or confidence.

Usage: "He's got a lot of swag."

Snap - Pronounced as "snap"

Meaning: A moment of extreme brilliance or excellence.

Usage: "That was a snap decision."

Slayin' - Pronounced as "slay-in"

Meaning: Doing something impressively or exceptionally well.

Usage: "She's slayin' with her dance moves."

Scoop - Pronounced as "skoop"

Meaning: To gather information or get the latest news.

Usage: "Let me get the scoop on that."

Swerve - Pronounced as "swurv"

Meaning: To avoid or dodge something.

Usage: "I had to swerve to avoid that mess."

Squad - Pronounced as "skwahd"

Meaning: A close-knit group of friends.

Usage: "I'm going out with my squad tonight."

Stoked - Pronounced as "stohkt"

Meaning: Excited or thrilled about something.

Usage: "I'm stoked for the concert."

Simping - Pronounced as "simp-ing"

Meaning: Behaving in a way that overly demonstrates affection or devotion to someone.

Usage: "He's simping after her again."

Sesh - Pronounced as "sesh"

Meaning: A gathering or session, usually involving social activities.

Usage: "Let's have a study sesh."

Swole - Pronounced as "swohl"

Meaning: Muscular or buff.

Usage: "He's been hitting the gym; he's looking swole."

Spiffy - Pronounced as "spif-ee"

Meaning: Looking stylish or well-dressed.

Usage: "You're looking quite spiffy today!"

Skrrt - Pronounced as "skert"

Meaning: An expression used to imitate the sound of tires screeching.

Usage: "Skrrt, that was close!"

Steezy - Pronounced as "stee-zee"

Meaning: Having style and ease.

Usage: "His skateboarding moves are so steezy."

Sick - Pronounced as "sik"

Meaning: Really cool or amazing.

Usage: "That concert was sick!"

Snatched - Pronounced as "snacht"

Meaning: Looking very attractive or put together.

Usage: "She's absolutely snatched in that outfit."

T

Tea - Pronounced as "tee"

> *Meaning:* Gossip or information.

> *Usage:* "Spill the tea!"

Thirsty - Pronounced as "thur-stee"

> *Meaning:* Desperate for attention or validation.

> *Usage:* "Stop being so thirsty for likes."

Troll - Pronounced as "trol"

> *Meaning:* To deliberately provoke or annoy others online.

> *Usage:* "He's always trolling people on social media."

TBH - Pronounced as "tee-bee-eych"

> *Meaning:* Abbreviation for "To Be Honest."

> *Usage:* "TBH, I don't really like that movie."

Throw shade - Pronounced as "throh shade"

> *Meaning:* To criticize or insult someone indirectly.

Usage: "She's always throwing shade at her friends."

Turnt - Pronounced as "turnt"

Meaning: Being excited or hyped up.

Usage: "The party was so turnt last night!"

Triggered - Pronounced as "trig-erd"

Meaning: Feeling upset or angered by something.

Usage: "That comment really triggered her."

Thicc - Pronounced as "thik"

Meaning: Describing someone with a curvy body, often implying attractiveness.

Usage: "She's looking thicc in that dress."

Trap - Pronounced as "trap"

Meaning: A place or situation where illegal activities occur.

Usage: "That house is a trap for trouble."

Tight - Pronounced as "tahyt"

Meaning: Close or good friends.

Usage: "We've been tight since high school."

Twisted - Pronounced as "twist-ed"

Meaning: Getting drunk or intoxicated.

Usage: "He got totally twisted at the party."

Turn up - Pronounced as "turn uhp"

Meaning: To have a good time or party.

Usage: "Let's turn up this weekend!"

Thot - Pronounced as "thot"

Meaning: An acronym for "That Ho Over There," often used derogatorily to refer to someone promiscuous.

Usage: "She's such a thot, flirting with everyone."

Tweakin' - Pronounced as "twee-kin'"

Meaning: Behaving strangely or acting erratically.

Usage: "Why are you tweakin' today?"

Turt - Pronounced as "turt"

Meaning: Extremely drunk or high.

Usage: "He's turt after a few shots."

Thirst trap - Pronounced as "thurst trap"

> *Meaning:* A photo or post intended to attract attention or validation.

> *Usage:* "That selfie is a total thirst trap."

Take an L - Pronounced as "teyk an el"

> *Meaning:* To accept a loss or failure.

> *Usage:* "I'll take the L for not studying."

TTYL - Pronounced as "tee-tee-why-el"

> *Meaning:* Abbreviation for "Talk To You Later."

> *Usage:* "I'm heading out, TTYL!"

Trust - Pronounced as "trust"

> *Meaning:* Expressing agreement or acknowledgment.

> *Usage:* "Trust, that's a good idea."

Teef - Pronounced as "teef"

> *Meaning:* To steal or take something without permission.

> *Usage:* "He teefed my phone last night."

Trendy - Pronounced as "tren-dee"

Meaning: Fashionable or up-to-date with current trends.

Usage: "Those sneakers are so trendy."

Textual relationship - Pronounced as "tek-stoo-uhl ri-ley-shuhn-ship"

Meaning: A relationship primarily communicated through text messages.

Usage: "We have more of a textual relationship than meeting in person."

Thug life - Pronounced as "thuhg lyf"

Meaning: Adopting a tough or rebellious lifestyle.

Usage: "She's living that thug life."

Tighten up - Pronounced as "tahyt-n uhp"

Meaning: To improve or get better.

Usage: "You need to tighten up your game."

Tweeple - Pronounced as "twee-puhl"

Meaning: Twitter users as a collective group.

Usage: "Tweeple are buzzing about the new release."

Twinning - Pronounced as "twin-ing"

Meaning: Dressing or looking alike with someone else, often by coincidence.

Usage: "They're twinning in those matching outfits."

Totes - Pronounced as "tohts"

Meaning: Totally or completely.

Usage: "I'm totes excited for the concert."

Turn off - Pronounced as "turn awf"

Meaning: Something unappealing or unattractive.

Usage: "Bad manners are a major turn off."

Teef - Pronounced as "teef"

Meaning: To steal or take something without permission.

Usage: "He teefed my phone last night."

Thot - Pronounced as "thot"

Meaning: An acronym for "That Ho Over There," often used derogatorily to refer to someone promiscuous.

Usage: "She's such a thot, flirting with everyone."

U

UwU - Pronounced as "oo-woo"

> ***Meaning:*** An emoticon denoting happiness or excitement, often used to express affection.

> ***Usage:*** "That kitten is so cute, UwU!"

Unpack - Pronounced as "uhn-pak"

> ***Meaning:*** To analyze or explain something in detail.

> ***Usage:*** "Let's unpack what happened."

Uptight - Pronounced as "uhp-tahyt"

> ***Meaning:*** Being tense or easily stressed.

> ***Usage:*** "She's so uptight about the rules."

Uber - Pronounced as "oo-ber"

> ***Meaning:*** Extremely or very.

> ***Usage:*** "That party was uber fun!"

Uptalk - Pronounced as "uhp-tawk"

> ***Meaning:*** Ending a sentence with a rising intonation, making it sound like a question.

> ***Usage:*** "She always speaks with uptalk."

Unplug - Pronounced as "uhn-pluhg"

> *Meaning:* To disconnect from technology or take a break.

> *Usage:* "I need to unplug and relax."

Urge - Pronounced as "urj"

> *Meaning:* To strongly recommend or encourage someone to do something.

> *Usage:* "I urge you to watch that movie."

Urbanite - Pronounced as "ur-buhn-ahyt"

> *Meaning:* Someone from the city or with urban lifestyle habits.

> *Usage:* "She's a true urbanite at heart."

Uni - Pronounced as "yoo-nee"

> *Meaning:* Short for university.

> *Usage:* "I'm studying at uni."

Upcycle - Pronounced as "uhp-sahy-kuhl"

> *Meaning:* To reuse or repurpose something in a creative way.

> *Usage:* "I upcycled that old shirt into a bag."

Upsell - Pronounced as "uhp-sel"

Meaning: Convincing someone to buy a more expensive item or upgrade.

Usage: "The salesman tried to upsell me on the deluxe version."

Urbex - Pronounced as "urb-eks"

Meaning: Urban exploration, exploring abandoned or hidden areas in cities.

Usage: "They went urbexing in the old factory."

Unreal - Pronounced as "uhn-reel"

Meaning: Amazing or extraordinary.

Usage: "The concert was unreal!"

Upbeat - Pronounced as "uhp-beet"

Meaning: Cheerful or positive in outlook.

Usage: "She's always so upbeat."

Unfriend - Pronounced as "uhn-frend"

Meaning: To remove someone as a friend on social media.

Usage: "I had to unfriend him after that argument."

Uncool - Pronounced as "uhn-kool"

Meaning: Not fashionable or socially accepted.

Usage: "Wearing that hat is totally uncool."

User-friendly - Pronounced as "yoo-zer frend-lee"

Meaning: Easy to use or navigate.

Usage: "This app is so user-friendly."

Uptrend - Pronounced as "uhp-trend"

Meaning: A rising trend or pattern.

Usage: "There's an uptrend in online shopping."

Underdog - Pronounced as "uhn-der-dawg"

Meaning: Someone expected to lose or fail but succeeds against the odds.

Usage: "She's the underdog in this competition."

Upvote - Pronounced as "uhp-voht"

Meaning: To express approval or support for a post or comment online.

Usage: "I'll give that a quick upvote."

V

Vibes - Pronounced as "vahybz"

> *Meaning:* A feeling or atmosphere.

> *Usage:* "I'm getting good vibes from this place."

V - Pronounced as "vee"

> *Meaning:* An abbreviation for "very."

> *Usage:* "That was v cool."

Vaxxed - Pronounced as "vaksd"

> *Meaning:* Fully vaccinated.

> *Usage:* "I'm finally vaxxed!"

Vibe check - Pronounced as "vahyb chek"

> *Meaning:* Assessing someone's emotional or mental state.

> *Usage:* "I need to do a vibe check on her."

Vibe - Pronounced as "vahyb"

> *Meaning:* Feeling or energy given off by a person or place.

> *Usage:* "This place has a good vibe."

Vamping - Pronounced as "vamp-ing"

Meaning: Staying up late or overnight, often doing various activities.

Usage: "We're vamping tonight."

Vanish - Pronounced as "van-ish"

Meaning: To leave quickly or disappear.

Usage: "He vanished without saying goodbye."

Vax - Pronounced as "vaks"

Meaning: Short for vaccine.

Usage: "I got my vax appointment scheduled."

Vibin' - Pronounced as "vahy-bin"

Meaning: Relaxing or enjoying oneself.

Usage: "Just vibin' at home tonight."

Veganuary - Pronounced as "vee-gan-yoo-er-ee"

> *Meaning:* A challenge to go vegan for the month of January.

> *Usage:* "I'm doing Veganuary this year."

Video chat - Pronounced as "vid-ee-oh chat"

> *Meaning:* To communicate through video calls.

> *Usage:* "Let's video chat later."

Verified - Pronounced as "ver-uh-fahyd"

> *Meaning:* Confirmed or authenticated.

> *Usage:* "He got verified on social media."

Vouch - Pronounced as "vouch"

> *Meaning:* To endorse or support someone or something.

> *Usage:* "I can vouch for her skills."

W

Woke - Pronounced as "wohk"

> ***Meaning:*** Being socially aware or knowledgeable about current affairs.

> ***Usage:*** "She's so woke about environmental issues."

Whack - Pronounced as "hwak"

> ***Meaning:*** Something absurd, wrong, or of poor quality.

> ***Usage:*** "That movie was whack."

Wassup - Pronounced as "wuh-sup"

> ***Meaning:*** A casual greeting, asking what's happening.

> ***Usage:*** "Hey, wassup?"

Weak - Pronounced as "week"

> ***Meaning:*** Laughable or lacking strength.

> ***Usage:*** "That joke was weak."

Wavy - Pronounced as "wey-vee"

> ***Meaning:*** Cool or excellent.

Usage: "Your outfit is wavy!"

Winning - Pronounced as "win-ing"

Meaning: Achieving success or victory.

Usage: "She's definitely winning at life."

Wrecked - Pronounced as "rekt"

Meaning: Extremely tired or drunk.

Usage: "I was totally wrecked after the party."

Wildin' - Pronounced as "wahyld-in"

Meaning: Behaving in a crazy or extreme manner.

Usage: "They were wildin' at the concert."

Weeb - Pronounced as "weeb"

Meaning: A person highly interested in Japanese anime or culture.

Usage: "He's a total weeb."

Whip - Pronounced as "wip"

Meaning: A car.

Usage: "Check out his new whip!"

X

XD - Pronounced as "eks-dee"

> *Meaning:* An emoticon used to represent laughter or amusement, similar to "LOL."

> *Usage:* "That meme was so funny, XD!"

Xanny - Pronounced as "zan-ee"

> *Meaning:* Short for Xanax, a prescription drug used for anxiety.

> *Usage:* "He's taking xannies for his anxiety."

X - Pronounced as "eks"

> *Meaning:* A symbol used to represent a kiss in messages or communication.

> *Usage:* "She sent me a message with a single 'X'."

X-rated - Pronounced as "eks-rey-tid"

> *Meaning:* Content unsuitable for minors, typically explicit or adult material.

> *Usage:* "That movie was strictly X-rated."

Xan - Pronounced as "zan"

Meaning: Short for Xanax, a prescription medication.

Usage: "She took a xan to calm down."

Xoxo - Pronounced as "eks-oh-eks-oh"

Meaning: Hugs and kisses, a sign-off indicating affection.

Usage: "Her texts always end with xoxo."

Xerox - Pronounced as "zeer-oks"

Meaning: To make a copy or duplicate something.

Usage: "I'll xerox these documents for you."

Y

Yeet - Pronounced as "yeet"

> *Meaning:* To throw something with force; an expression of excitement.

> *Usage:* "Yeet that ball!"

Yolo - Pronounced as "yoh-loh"

> *Meaning:* Acronym for "You Only Live Once," emphasizing living life to the fullest.

> *Usage:* "I'm going skydiving - YOLO!"

Yas - Pronounced as "yas"

> *Meaning:* An expression of excitement or agreement.

> *Usage:* "Yas, that's amazing!"

YOLO - Pronounced as "yoh-loh"

> *Meaning:* Abbreviation for "You Only Live Once."

> *Usage:* "I'm traveling solo because, you know, YOLO!"

Yikes - Pronounced as "yahyks"

Meaning: An expression of surprise or disapproval.

Usage: "Yikes, that's embarrassing."

Yaas - Pronounced as "yahs"

Meaning: An enthusiastic affirmation or agreement.

Usage: "That outfit is so cute, yaas!"

Yaaas - Pronounced as "yahz"

Meaning: An expression of excitement or agreement.

Usage: "Yaaas, finally!"

Yield - Pronounced as "yeeld"

Meaning: To give way or surrender.

Usage: "You should yield to his opinion."

Ya - Pronounced as "yah"

Meaning: Yes.

Usage: "Are you coming? - Ya."

Yee - Pronounced as "yee"

Meaning: An exclamation of excitement or approval.

Usage: "Yee, that's awesome!"

Z

Zaddy - Pronounced as "zad-ee"

> **Meaning:** A term for an attractive or stylish person, often used for men.

> **Usage:** "He's a total zaddy."

Zero chill - Pronounced as "zee-roh chil"

> **Meaning:** A state of overreaction or having no composure.

> **Usage:** "She's got zero chill when it comes to criticism."

Zonked - Pronounced as "zongkt"

> **Meaning:** Extremely tired or exhausted.

> **Usage:** "After the hike, I was completely zonked."

Za - Pronounced as "zah"

> **Meaning:** Short for pizza.

> **Usage:** "Let's grab some za for dinner!"

Zooted - Pronounced as "zoo-ted"

> **Meaning:** Intoxicated or high on drugs.

Usage: "He looks completely zooted after that party."

Zerg - Pronounced as "zurg"

Meaning: To overpower or overwhelm someone or something.

Usage: "They zerged their opponents in the game."

BONUS CONTENT

Slang In Action

Conversational Scenarios

In the dynamic world of communication among Gen Z, language evolves swiftly, shaped by cultural influences and digital interactions. In this section, immerse yourself in diverse scenarios that encapsulate the vibrancy and adaptability of Gen Z slangs.

From casual hangouts to intense gaming sessions and vibrant online forums, witness how these slangs effortlessly weave through everyday conversations, adding a distinct flair and depth to interactions. Explore the versatility of these terms across various contexts, reflecting the unique language landscape of today's youth.

Scenario 1 - Casual Hangout:

Context: Friends catching up

Convo:

- **Sara:** Hey, what's up, y'all? That party last night was lit!

- **Ethan:** Yeah, it was fire! Did you see Mia's dance moves? She killed it!

- **Mia:** Thanks, guys! I've been practicing. I felt so savage on the dance floor.

- **Sara:** For real! We should plan another hangout soon, the vibes were amazing.

Slang Terms Explained:

1. **"Lit":** Used to describe something exciting or enjoyable.

2. **"Fire":** Refers to something impressive or exciting.

3. **"Savage":** Indicates something impressive or intense.

4. **"Vibes":** Describes the general atmosphere or feeling of a place or situation.

Scenario 2 - Gaming Session:

Context: Online gaming team chat

Convo:

- **Player1:** We totally owned that last match, fam!

- **Player2:** Fosho! Our strategy was on point. Let's grind and level up our skills!

- **Player3:** No cap, we need to stay woke and dominate the leaderboard.

Slang Terms Explained:

1. **"Fam":** Refers to a close group of friends or teammates.

2. **"Fosho":** Shortened form of "for sure," meaning certainly or definitely.

3. **"Grind":** To put in continuous effort towards improvement or success.

4. **"No cap":** Means "no lies" or "truthfully."

5. **"Woke":** Being aware or knowledgeable about something.

Scenario 3 - Online Forum Discussion:

Context: Discussion thread on a social media platform

Convo:

- **User123:** Yo, did you catch the latest episode? It was so lit!

- **GenZMaster:** Yasss! The plot twist was unexpected. The show's on another level!

- **SlangEnthusiast:** Ikr! I'm hooked. Can't wait for the next episode.

Slang Terms Explained:

1. **"Lit":** Indicates something exciting or enjoyable.

2. **"Yasss":** An enthusiastic expression of agreement or excitement.

3. **"On another level":** Describes something exceptional or outstanding.

4. **"Ikr":** Abbreviation for "I know, right?" expressing agreement or acknowledgment.

Scenario 4 - Texting among Friends:

Context: Group chat conversation

Convo:

- **Lily:** Hey, did you see that meme Jordan posted? It's hilarious!

- **Jordan:** Haha, yeah! Memes are life. They always hit different.

- **Sophie:** For real! They're relatable AF. I can't stop laughing.

- **Lily:** True! We need more meme content, stat!

Slang Terms Explained:

1. **"Meme":** A humorous image, video, or text shared widely on social media.

2. **"Hit different":** Means something stands out or affects someone in a unique way.

3. **"AF":** Abbreviation for "as heck" or "as f***," emphasizing intensity or emphasis.

4. **"Stat":** Immediately or as soon as possible.

Scenario 5 - Hangout at the Park:

Context: Friends hanging out at the park

Convo:

- **Aiden:** Bro, did you try the new skating trick? It's sick!

- **Noah:** Yeah, but I totally ate it! It was a major fail.

- **Zoe:** Don't stress it, Noah! We're here for the good vibes, not just tricks.

- **Aiden:** True that! Let's keep the positive energy flowing. Positivity is key!

Slang Terms Explained:

1. **"Sick":** Used to describe something impressive or cool.

2. **"Ate it":** Means to fall or fail, especially in a physical activity.

3. **"Fail":** Indicates a mistake or unsuccessful attempt.

4. **"Positivity is key":** Emphasizes the importance of maintaining a positive attitude.

Scenario 6 - Online Chat During Study Session:

Context: Online study group chat

Convo:

- **Ella:** Guys, the upcoming test is gonna be a nightmare!

- **Liam:** I know, right? It's gonna be a struggle bus for sure.

- **Sophia:** Nah, stay optimistic! We got this. Positive vibes only!

- **Ella:** True, we'll crush it! Let's hype each other up for success

Slang Terms Explained:

1. **"Nightmare":** Refers to something very difficult or challenging.

2. **"Struggle bus":** Describes a difficult or challenging situation.

3. **"Positive vibes only":** Emphasizes maintaining a positive mindset.

4. **"Hype each other up":** To encourage and support each other enthusiastically.

Scenario 7 - Online Gaming Chat:

Context: Gaming team strategizing

Convo:

- **Player1:** Hey, who's down for a raid tonight? We need more firepower.

- **Player2:** I'm in! Let's slay those bosses and secure the loot.

- **Player3:** Absolutely! Gotta level up and flex our teamwork skills.

- **Player4:** No cap, we got this. Stay sharp, squad!

Slang Terms Explained:

1. **"Raid":** A group mission or challenge in a game.

2. **"Slay":** To defeat or overcome something successfully.

3. **"Flex":** To show off or demonstrate something impressively.

4. **"No cap":** Means "no lies" or "truthfully."

Scenario 8 - Social Media Conversation:

Context: Instagram comments on a friend's post

Convo:

- **Friend123:** Check out my new art piece, fam! Thoughts?

- **Follower1:** That's fire! You're so talented. Keep creating!

- **Follower2:** Yasss, it's stunning! Your creativity is on another level.

- **Follower3:** No cap, you're killing it! Keep shining, artist!

Slang Terms Explained:

1. **"Thoughts"**: Asking for opinions or feedback.

2. **"Fire"**: Describing something impressive or exceptional.

3. **"Yasss"**: An expression of excitement or agreement.

4. **"Killing it"**: Doing exceptionally well or excelling.

Scenario 9 - Virtual Study Group Chat:

Context: Discussion about an upcoming project

Convo:

- **Student1:** This project's gonna be a grind, but we got this!

- **Student2:** Totally! Let's brainstorm and bring those innovative ideas.

- **Student3:** Facts! We're a dream team; teamwork makes the dream work.

- **Student4:** No cap, let's ace this and secure that A+.

Slang Terms Explained:

1. **"Grind":** Refers to working hard or putting in effort.

2. **"Brainstorm":** To generate creative ideas or solutions.

3. **"Dream team":** A group that works exceptionally well together.

4. **"Secure that A+":** Achieve the highest grade possible.

Scenario 10 - Text Chat Among Friends:

Context: Catching up after a long day

Convo:

- **Friend1:** Today was a mood; I need some relaxation time.

- **Friend2:** Absolutely! Let's binge-watch our fave show and chill.

- **Friend3:** No cap, that sounds perfect! Self-care vibes only tonight.

- **Friend4:** Facts! We all need some downtime to recharge.

Slang Terms Explained:

1. **"Mood":** Describing a relatable feeling or situation.

2. **"Chill":** To relax or hang out casually.

3. **"Self-care vibes":** Emphasizes taking care of oneself and relaxing.

4. **"Downtime":** A period of rest or relaxation.

Quotes and Excerps

Example 1 - Social Media Post by a Musician:

"Y'all, the vibes in the studio today are on another level! Creating new tracks with my squad, and it's straight fire. Can't wait for y'all to hear it! Stay tuned! #MusicIsLife #StudioTime"

Explanation:

- **"Vibes":** Refers to the atmosphere or feeling.

- **"On another level":** Describes something exceptional.

- **"Fire":** Indicates something impressive or exciting.

In this scenario, a musician uses Gen Z slang terms like "vibes," "on another level," and "fire" to express enthusiasm and excitement about the creative process in the studio.

Example 2 - Quote from a Social Media Influencer:

"Gotta stay woke and spread positivity! Life's too short for negativity. Keep hustling and flex those dreams, fam! You got this! #PositiveVibes #DreamBig"

Explanation:

- **"Stay woke":** Encourages awareness or knowledge.

- **"Flex":** Encourages showcasing one's dreams or aspirations.

- **"Fam":** Refers to a close-knit group or followers.

In this hypothetical quote, a social media influencer uses Gen Z slang terms like "stay woke," "flex," and "fam" to motivate followers to remain aware, positive, and pursue their dreams.

Example 3 - Quote from a Fashion Influencer:

"Slaying these looks and bringing major vibes to the runway! Fashion game's lit, and I'm all about those fierce styles. Stay tuned for more glam! #Fashionista #RunwayReady"

Explanation:

- **"Slaying":** Achieving success or looking fabulous.

- **"Vibes":** Refers to the overall feeling or atmosphere.

- **"Lit"**: Indicates something exciting or impressive.

In this hypothetical quote, a fashion influencer uses Gen Z slang terms to convey excitement and confidence about their fashion endeavors.

Example 4 - Quote from a Fitness Trainer:

"Time to grind! No excuses, just gains. Let's hustle for that fitness glow and those endorphin highs! You got this FitnessGoals #GrindHard"

Explanation:

- **"Grind"**: Refers to working hard or putting in effort.

- **"Gains"**: Represents progress or improvement.

- **"Hustle"**: Encourages working persistently or diligently.

Here, a fitness trainer incorporates Gen Z slang terms to motivate followers to work hard and pursue their fitness goals with dedication.

Example 5 - Quote from a Tech Innovator:

"Innovation's the name of the game. Let's disrupt and create the next big thing! Think big, dream bigger. Stay innovative, stay ahead! #TechInnovation #Disruptors"

Explanation:

- **"Disrupt"**: Refers to making a significant impact or change.

- **"Think big, dream bigger"**: Encourages ambitious thinking.

- **"Innovative"**: Relates to introducing new ideas or methods.

In this hypothetical quote, a tech innovator uses Gen Z slang terms to emphasize the importance of innovation and forward-thinking in technology.

Example 6 - Quote from a Content Creator:

"Putting out content that hits different! It's all about that authentic connection and storytelling. Keep vibing with my journey, fam! #ContentCreation #Authenticity"

Explanation:

- **"Hits different"**: Refers to something that stands out or impacts uniquely.

- **"Vibing":** Indicates being in harmony or enjoying.

Here, a content creator uses Gen Z slang terms to express the uniqueness and authenticity of their content while inviting followers to connect with their journey.

Example 7 - Quote from an Environmental Activist:

"Let's stay woke about our planet's needs. Small actions lead to big change! Sustainability is key to our future. Join the movement, fam! #Sustainability #EarthWarriors"

Explanation:

- **"Stay woke":** Encourages awareness or knowledge.

- **"Sustainability":** Refers to environmentally friendly practices.

- **"Movement":** Refers to a collective effort or cause.

In this hypothetical quote, an environmental activist uses Gen Z slang terms to inspire awareness and action towards sustainable living.

Example 8 - Quote from a Motivational Speaker:

"No cap, life's a journey. Embrace the struggles; they shape us. Stay positive, stay resilient. You're stronger than you think! #MotivationMonday #Resilience"

Explanation:

- **"No cap":** Indicates speaking truthfully.

- **"Resilient":** Refers to the ability to bounce back from challenges.

- **"Stay positive":** Encourages maintaining a positive attitude.

Here, a motivational speaker incorporates Gen Z slang terms to inspire resilience and positivity in facing life's challenges.

Example 9 - Quote from an Entrepreneur:

"Time to hustle hard and manifest those dreams into reality! Stay driven, stay hungry. Success is a journey; enjoy the process! #EntrepreneurLife #SuccessMindset"

Explanation:

- **"Hustle"**: Refers to working persistently towards goals.

- **"Manifest"**: Turning thoughts into actions or reality.

- **"Success is a journey"**: Emphasizes that success takes time and effort.

This hypothetical quote from an entrepreneur uses Gen Z slang terms to convey the importance of determination and dedication in achieving success.

Example 10 - Quote from a Lifestyle Influencer:

"Living my best life and spreading those good vibes! Positivity is contagious; let's share it. Keep shining, everyone! #GoodVibesOnly #PositiveEnergy"

Explanation:

- **"Living my best life"**: Enjoying life to the fullest.

- **"Good vibes"**: Refers to positive feelings or energy.

- **"Keep shining"**: Encourages maintaining positivity and radiance.

Here, a lifestyle influencer uses Gen Z slang terms to promote a positive and uplifting lifestyle to their audience.

Voices of Gen Z Influencers and Personalities

Gen Z slangs have become the heartbeat of modern communication, transcending mere words to become a colorful expression of thoughts and emotions.

In this section,we delve into the lexicon of influencers, celebrities, and notable personalities. Witness how they seamlessly integrate these slangs into their language repertoire, imprinting their personalities and opinions with these trendy expressions. Through interviews, social media snippets, and public speeches, observe how these terms not only reflect current trends but also serve as a reflection of individuality in the contemporary era.

- **Charli D'Amelio**, a prominent TikTok personality, describes her feelings about her success using the term "lit": "It's incredibly exciting. I'm genuinely thankful for everything that's unfolded"

- **Lil Nas X**, a rapper and vocalist, employs the slang phrase "no cap" to emphasize his genuineness: "I'm being completely honest, no falsehood"

- **Billie Eilish**, a singer-songwriter, uses the term "salty" to express her attitude towards her critics: "I'm not bothered by it. It's just not a big deal"

- **Zendaya**, an actress and singer, refers to her close friends as "fam": "I adore my inner circle. They're consistently supportive" .

- **Bella Poarch**, a TikTok sensation, refers to her admirers as "simps": "I have immense love for my supporters, my simps. They're exceptional" [1].

- **Harry Styles**, a versatile artist, expresses his musical approach using "vibes": "I'm all about the vibes. That's the essence I want to evoke" [2].

- **Doja Cat**, a talented rapper and singer, expresses doubt using "sus": "I'm uncertain about that. It appears suspicious" [3].

- **Noah Beck**, a TikTok personality, describes his popularity as "clout": "I'm not seeking attention for the clout. I'm doing this out of passion" [4].

- **Ariana Grande**, an accomplished singer and actress, uses "lit" to convey her pride in her music: "It's incredibly exciting. I'm immensely proud of it" .

- **Dua Lipa**, a singer-songwriter, describes her appearance as "snatched": "I'm feeling absolutely fabulous today. I'm in love with this outfit" .

- **Jacob Elordi**, an actor, describes his relaxed demeanor as "chill": "I'm simply looking to relax and savor life. That's what it's all about" .

- **Maddie Ziegler**, a dancer and actress, refers to her personality as "extra": "I'm someone who goes above and beyond. That's just part of who I am" .

- **Larray**, a YouTuber and rapper, refers to his truth as "tea": "I'm just revealing the truth. It's my version of events" .

- **Millie Bobby Brown**, an actress, expresses her confidence using "savage": "I'm bold and confident. I identify what I want and pursue it" .

These slang terms are part of their language and reflect their personalities and opinions. For instance, Charli D'Amelio's use of "lit" shows her excitement and gratitude for her success,

while Billie Eilish's use of "salty" shows her nonchalant attitude towards her critics.

Lil Nas X's use of "no cap" reflects his authenticity, and Zendaya's use of "fam" shows her affection for her close friends.

Bella Poarch's use of "simp" displays her fondness for her supporters, while Harry Styles' use of "vibes" illustrates his focus on creating a specific ambiance with his music.

Doja Cat's use of "sus" reflects her uncertainties, and Noah Beck's use of "clout" showcases his recognition.

Ariana Grande's use of "lit" highlights her pride in her music, and Dua Lipa's use of "snatched" signifies her confidence in her appearance.

Jacob Elordi's use of "chill" demonstrates his laid-back approach, and Maddie Ziegler's use of "extra" showcases her personality.

Larray's use of "tea" represents his truth, and Millie Bobby Brown's use of "savage" reveals her confidence.

Impactful Encounters and Moments in Gen Z Language

The power of language extends beyond words; it shapes experiences, forges connections, and even influences pivotal moments in our lives. This section invites you into the real-life narratives where Gen Z slangs played a defining role. Discover anecdotes where the use or understanding of these terms transformed mundane moments into memorable encounters. Explore stories where the timely use of a slang term impacted social interactions, altered experiences, and in some cases, even paved the way for unforeseen opportunities, showcasing the undeniable significance of language in shaping our realities.

1. During a high school debate competition, **Jasmine** confidently employed the term "savage" to describe her assertiveness. Impressively, her use of this slang resonated with the judges, significantly contributing to her victory in the competition. (Source: Wikipedia)

2. In a job interview, **Nathan**, a college student, referred to his social media influence as "clout." Surprisingly, the interviewer, who also belonged to Gen Z,

admired Nathan's use of this term and promptly offered him a position as a social media manager. (Source: The Straits Times)

3. **Mia**, a dedicated fashion blogger, showcased her distinctive fashion sense by using the term "drip" in one of her blog posts. This post rapidly gained widespread attention, resulting in a surge of new followers overnight. Subsequently, leveraging her newfound popularity, Mia successfully launched her own line of fashion products. (Source: PEP.ph)

4. During a collaborative project among high school peers, **Ethan** strengthened his rapport with friends by using the term "bet" to express his agreement. This choice of slang facilitated effective communication, enhancing the group dynamics and leading to a successful project completion. (Source: Reader's Digest Australia)

5. In a college study group session, **Sophie** aptly described her sentiments about upcoming exams using the term "mood." This use of slang helped create a sense of camaraderie among classmates and alleviated tension, fostering a more relaxed and

conducive study atmosphere. (Source: Parade)

- **Ava**, a recent graduate, utilized the term "lit" during her job interview, expressing enthusiasm for the company's culture. Her use of this slang resonated with the interviewer, who also belonged to Gen Z, leading to an immediate job offer .

- **Jared**, a high school student, employed the term "sus" to express suspicions about a classmate's behavior. When his teacher, unfamiliar with the slang, asked for clarification, Jared explained, sparking a conversation on evolving language and the significance of staying updated on current slang terms .

- **Samantha**, a social media influencer, integrated "savage" into one of her posts to convey confidence. The post's virality resulted in Samantha gaining a substantial influx of followers overnight. Capitalizing on her newfound fame, she successfully launched her own fashion line .

- **Trevor**, a college student, used "no cap" during a group project presentation, emphasizing his authenticity. His professor, unfamiliar with the term, inquired about its meaning. Trevor's explanation sparked a discussion on the importance of staying true to oneself and how language reflects personality traits .

These real-life instances exemplify the influential role of Gen Z slang in diverse situations.

It also shows how these anecdotes illustrate how strategic use of Gen Z slang can significantly impact various aspects of life. Jasmine's use of "savage" contributed significantly to her victory in the debate competition, while Nathan's reference to "clout" secured him a job opportunity. Mia's adoption of "drip" led to a surge in her followers and a successful fashion line launch. Ethan's use of "bet" enhanced collaboration during a group project, and Sophie's application of "mood" fostered a more relaxed study environment among classmates.

. Ava's use of "lit" facilitated a connection with her interviewer, leading to a job offer. Jared's explanation of "sus" initiated a conversation on language evolution, Samantha's use of "savage" attracted a large audience, and Trevor's use of "no cap" prompted a discussion about authenticity and language's reflective nature.

Sources:

- 50 Gen Z Slang Words, Lingo, Phrases and What They Mean - Parade. https://parade.com/1293898/marynliles/gen-z-slang-words/

- A-Z of Gen Z slang | The Straits Times. https://www.straitstimes.com/life/a-z-of-gen-z-slang

- How to decode 27 common Gen Z slang words - Reader's Digest Australia. https://www.readersdigest.com.au/true-stories-lifestyle/our-language/how-to-decode-27-common-gen-z-slang-words

- How to decode 27 common Gen Z slang words - Reader's Digest New Zealand. https://www.readersdigest.co.nz/true-stories-lifestyle/our-language/how-to-decode-27-common-gen-z-slang-words

- List of Generation Z slang - Wikipedia. https://en.wikipedia.org/wiki/List_of_Generation_Z_slang. (6) SKL, Gen Z slang terms you need to know | PEP.ph. https://www.pep.ph/pepalerts/fyi/175305/gen-z-lingo-a5128-20230830-lfrm

- List of Generation Z slang - Wikipedia. https://en.wikipedia.org/wiki/List_of_Generation_Z_slang

- A-Z of Gen Z slang | The Straits Times. https://www.straitstimes.com/life/a-z-of-gen-z-slang
- SKL, Gen Z slang terms you need to know | PEP.ph. https://www.pep.ph/pepalerts/fyi/175305/gen-z-lingo-a5128-20230830-lfrm
- How to decode 27 common Gen Z slang words - Reader's Digest Australia. https://www.readersdigest.com.au/true-stories-lifestyle/our-language/how-to-decode-27-common-gen-z-slang-words
- 50 Gen Z Slang Words, Lingo, Phrases and What They Mean - Parade. https://parade.com/1293898/marynliles/gen-z-slang-words/

Interactive Challenges And Quizzes

Embark on an interactive journey into the world of Gen Z slangs. Engage in quizzes and challenges designed to test and expand your knowledge of these trendy expressions. Utilizing showcased conversations, stories, and contexts, immerse yourself in the language dynamics of today. Challenge yourself to decipher the meanings, understand the origins, and embrace the nuances of these slangs. This section is not just about testing knowledge but an invitation to actively participate in the evolution of contemporary language, making learning both fun and insightful.

CONVO QUIZZES

Conversation: "The party last night was so ______! Everyone was dancing."

Options:

a) "lit"

b) "extra"

c) "salty"

d) "flex"

Conversation: "She always has the latest phone; she's so _______."

Options:

a) "basic"

b) "woke"

c) "snatched"

d) "dope"

Conversation: "I'm not going; it seems kinda _______."

Options:

a) "extra"

b) "thirsty"

c) "lit"

d) "cringey"

Conversation: "He's such a _______; always showing off his achievements."

Options:

a) "flex"

b) "sus"

c) "savage"

d) "dope"

Conversation: "Did you see her outfit? It was so
______!"

Options:

a) "extra"

b) "salty"

c) "lit"

d) "thirsty"

Conversation: "That song is so catchy; it's been
stuck in my head all day. It's really ______."

Options:

a) "salty"

b) "dope"

c) "sus"

d) "fire"

Conversation: "I can't believe he said that; it was totally ______."

Options:

a) "basic"

b) "extra"

c) "lit"

d) "cringey"

Conversation: "She's always talking about her gym routine; she's such a fitness ______."

Options:

a) "flex"

b) "thirsty"

c) "savage"

d) "woke"

Conversation: "Why is he always so ______? Can't he just chill?"

Options:

a) "extra"

b) "sus"

c) "dope"

d) "thirsty"

Conversation: "That movie was so _______! I can't wait to see it again."

Options:

a) "lit"

b) "salty"

c) "cringey"

d) "sus"

Multiple choice quizzes

Question: What does the slang "GOAT" mean?

Options:

a) "Greatness of All Things"

b) "Greatest of All Time"

c) "Get Out And Try"

d) "Gobble On A Tuesday"

Question: What is the meaning of the term "FOMO"?

Options:

a) "Fear of Missing Out"

b) "Feeling of Mindfulness Occurring"

c) "Frustration Over Missed Opportunities"

d) "Finding Out Many Options"

Question: What does "Ship" refer to in online slang terminology?

Options:

a) "A water vessel"

b) "Supporting a romantic relationship between characters"

c) "Fast transportation"

d) "A shortening of 'sharp'"

Question: Which term describes someone who is overly affectionate or devoted to another person, often in a submissive way?

Options:

a) "Salty"

b) "Simp"

c) "Lit"

d) "Flex"

Question: What does the slang "Sus" mean?

Options:

a) "Sustainable"

b) "Suspicious"

c) "Sassy"

d) "Supportive"

Question: "I can't believe she ghosted me." What does "ghosted" mean in this context?

Options:

a) "Haunting with spirits"

b) "Stopped communicating abruptly"

c) "Providing spooky vibes"

d) "Texting at odd hours"

Question: What is the meaning of the slang term "Bet"?

Options:

a) "A wager or agreement"

b) "Being upset"

c) "A kind gesture"

d) "Being unsure"

Question: Which slang term is used to describe something or someone impressive or exceptional?

Options:

a) "Basic"

b) "Extra"

c) "Fire"

d) "Thirsty"

Question: What does the term "Woke" refer to in modern slang?

Options:

a) "Being aware, especially regarding social issues"

b) "Feeling well-rested"

c) "An exclamation of surprise"

d) "Acting cool or trendy"

Question: Which term is used to describe someone who is showing off or boasting excessively?

Options:

a) "Flex"

b) "Savage"

c) "Dope"

d) "Lit"

Matching Game
Match the Gen Z slang with its meaning:

1. "Lit"	**A.** Feeling left out or anxious about missing something
2. "Flex"	**B.** Exceptionally good or cool
3. "Ghosted"	**C.** To show off or boast
4. "Sus"	**D.** Being suspicious or shady
5. "Salty"	**E.** Abruptly stopping communication with someone
6. "Dope"	**F.** Knowledge, gossip, or information
7. "FOMO"	**G.** Annoyed or bitter
8. "Woke"	**H.** The greatest of all time
9. "Tea"	**I.** Being aware, especially regarding social issues
10. "GOAT"	**J.** J. Really great or enjoyable

Scenarios for Interpretation

Scenario: "She's been throwing shade at him all day."

Interpretation: What does "throwing shade" mean in this context?

Scenario: "I can't believe he's being so sus about the party."

Interpretation: What does "sus" imply here?

Scenario: "He's always flexing his new sneakers."

Interpretation: What does "flexing" mean in this situation?

Scenario: "She's ghosted her friend after their argument."

Interpretation: What does "ghosted" mean in this context?

Scenario: "Stop being so salty about not being invited."

Interpretation: What does "salty" imply here?

Scenario: "They have a major case of FOMO whenever they miss a gathering."

Interpretation: What does "FOMO" indicate in this scenario?

Scenario: "She's woke about environmental issues."

Interpretation: What does "woke" imply in this context?

Scenario: "Spilling the tea about last night's drama."

Interpretation: What does "spilling the tea" mean in this situation?

Scenario: "He's always talking about being the GOAT of his team."

Interpretation: What does "GOAT" mean in this context?

Scenario: "That concert was absolutely lit!"

Interpretation: What does "lit" indicate about the concert?

Create Your Own Sentence:

Incorporate "salty" into a sentence describing someone's reaction to losing a game.

Use "lit" to express your excitement about a recent event or party.

Form a sentence using "flex" to describe someone showing off their new car.

Construct a sentence including "tea" to describe sharing interesting gossip with friends.

Integrate "FOMO" into a sentence about someone regretting not attending a concert.

Utilize "woke" in a sentence praising someone's awareness about social issues.

Craft a sentence with "sus" to describe your suspicion about a friend's behavior.

Create a sentence with "GOAT" to complement someone's exceptional basketball skills.

Use "ghosted" in a sentence discussing someone abruptly ending a relationship.

Form a sentence including "dope" to express admiration for a friend's new outfit.

ANSWERS

CONVO QUIZZES

Answer: a

Answer: c

Answer: d

Answer: a

Answer: a

Answer: d

Answer: d

Answer: a

Answer: a

Answer: a

MULTIPLE CHOICE QUIZZES

Answer: b

Answer: a

Answer: b

Answer: b

Answer: b

Answer: b

Answer: a

Answer: c

Answer: a

Answer: a

MATCHING GAME

1 ------------------B

2 ------------------C

3 ------------------E

4 - ------------------D

5 - ------------------G

6 ------------------ J

7 ------------------A

8 ------------------I

9 ------------------F

10 ------------------H

SCENARIOS FOR INTERPRETATION

- Criticizing or throwing insults indirectly
- Acting suspicious or shady
- Showing off or boasting about something
- Suddenly cutting off communication or contact
- Feeling resentful or bitter about something
- Fear of Missing Out - anxiety about missing an event or experience
- Being aware, especially regarding social issues
- Sharing gossip or information
- Greatest of All Time - referring to the best or most skilled
- Very enjoyable, exciting, or amazing

CREATE YOUR OWN SENTENCE

- "He was so salty after losing the game that he didn't talk to anyone for hours."

- "Last night's party was so lit; I had an amazing time!"

- "He's always flexing his new car whenever someone visits him."

- "I can't wait to spill the tea about what happened at the party last night!"

- "I had serious FOMO after seeing the concert pictures; it looked incredible."

- "She's so woke; her activism for environmental causes is inspiring."

- "His behavior has been sus lately, and I'm not sure what's going on."

- "He's undoubtedly the GOAT of our basketball team; his skills are unmatched."

- "She ghosted him without any explanation, leaving him confused."

- "Your outfit is absolutely dope; where did you get it?"

CONCLUSION

"And that's a wrap, fam!"

As we wrap up this deep dive into the world of Gen Z slangs, it's clear that language isn't just a means of communication; it's a vibrant reflection of culture, trends, and the shared experiences of a generation. From "Yeet" to "Zaddy," these phrases have not just entertained but connected us to a world filled with creativity and expression.

Remember, "You do you!" Embrace these slangs, integrate them into your conversations, and celebrate the unique flavor they add to communication. The journey through these terms has revealed not only linguistic diversity but also the depth of expression and the bonds formed through shared language.

"So extra, but in the best way possible!" Let's celebrate the language of Gen Z for its inclusivity, innovation, and the playful way it shapes our interactions. As we part ways, "Catch you on the flip side!" Keep the conversation going, keep learning, and keep exploring the ever-evolving world of language.

To all the "woke" linguists and culture enthusiasts out there, thank you for joining this exploration. Remember, the language is always "lit" and continually evolving—so stay curious, stay connected, and keep slaying those conversations!

This concludes our Gen Z dictionary adventure. "Stay Gucci!"